INTRODUCTION

Welcome to the world of digital publishing ~ the book you now hold in your hand, while unchanged from the original edition, was printed using the latest state of the art digital technology. The advent of print-on-demand has forever changed the publishing process, never has information been so accessible and it is our hope that this book serves your informational needs for years to come. If this is your first exposure to digital publishing, we hope that you are pleased with the results. Many more titles of interest to the classic automobile and motorcycle enthusiast, collector and restorer are available via our website at **www.VelocePress.com**. We hope that you find this title as interesting as we do.

NOTE FROM THE PUBLISHER

The information presented is true and complete to the best of our knowledge. All recommendations are made without any guarantees on the part of the author or the publisher, who also disclaim all liability incurred with the use of this information.

TRADEMARKS

We recognize that some words, model names and designations, for example, mentioned herein are the property of the trademark holder. We use them for identification purposes only. This is not an official publication.

INFORMATION ON THE USE OF THIS PUBLICATION

In today's information age we are constantly subject to changes in common practice, new technology, availability of improved materials and increased awareness of chemical toxicity. As such, it is advised that the user consult with an experienced professional prior to undertaking any procedure described herein. While every care has been taken to ensure correctness of information, it is obviously not possible to guarantee complete freedom from errors or omissions or to accept liability arising from such errors or omissions. Therefore, any individual that uses the information contained within, or elects to perform or participate in do-it-yourself repairs or modifications acknowledges that there is a risk factor involved and that the publisher or its associates cannot be held responsible for personal injury or property damage resulting from the use of the information or the outcome of such procedures.

It is important that the reader recognizes that any instructions may refer to either the right-hand or left-hand sides of the vehicle or the components and that the directions are followed carefully. One final word of advice, this publication is intended to be used as a reference guide, and when in doubt the reader should consult with a qualified technician.

CONTENTS

Compiled from the **Floyd Clymer** book, titled **"Handbook of Imported Carburetors & Fuel Injection"**, this publication is specific to the **45 DCOE, 40 DCOE, 26 IMB, 22 IM, 26 IM, 28 ICP, 28 ICI, 32 IMPE, 36 DCD and 28/36 DCD** series of **Weber** carburetors.

The book is split into two sections, the first section deals with the "Theory and Practice" of this series of carburetors and the second section focuses on the installation, tune up and maintenance of those carburetors as fitted to the Alfa Romeo Giulia 1600 models, including the TI Super and Sprint GT Sedan, the 1600 Spider, Veloce and GT. In addition, Weber carburetors fitted to the Fiat 500, 600, 1100, 1200 and 1500 Cabriolet are covered in detail.

INDEX

WEBER Carburetors – Theory & Practice .... Page 1

ALFA ROMEO .... Page 53

FIAT .... Page 69

WEBER Special Tools .... Page 110

While there are certainly other books that deal with current Weber products, detailed information on these earlier carburetors is more difficult to find. Obviously, in addition to Alfa Romeo and Fiat automobiles, much of the information in this publication will be applicable to other vehicles that are equipped with similar Weber carburetion systems. Therefore, we believe this book is an important addition to any enthusiast's library and will help keep their Weber equipped automobiles in top operating condition.

WEBER CARBURETORS
THEORY
AND PRACTICE

WEBER CARBURETORS

Basically, the carburetor consists of:
1) **Idle speed and progression circuit**
2) **Main fuel feed circuit**
3) **Starting device or starter.**

It is important to point out that a normally adjusted carburetor represents a compromise solution which on the whole meets the requirements of the engine. When any of its factory-set adjustments are modified, its functionality will inevitably be upset to a degree seldom justified by the improvements sought.

For instance, sometimes it is possible to increase the top speed of a car by fitting a larger-diameter venturi and a suitable main jet: in this case, however, it will be found that slow running operation is slightly worsened.

Before any such modification, one should first consider if the desired improvement justifies the consequent faulty performance. This example confirms the above outlined assertion that a well-adjusted carburetor is invariably the best possible compromise between pick-up performance, fuel consumption and vehicle speed.

When an engine **idles,** that is, the car is at a standstill and engine turns over at around **450-600 rpm,** the vacuum promoted under these conditions in the venturi area is too weak to draw out any mixture through the spray nozzle, but this is handled by a small independent carburetor whose task is to give the engine a mixture in the amount and strength required to ensure smooth engine operation at low rotational speeds, at the same time developing just the power needed to overcome the resistance of the moving parts.

As a matter of fact, the three basic elements into which carburetors were divided in a previous paragraph are actually three complete and independent carburetors sharing in common a constant-level bowl for their fuel supply.

This usually holds true even when—as will be outlined later—the idle speed circuit does not derive its fuel supply directly from the bowl but from a well.

It then follows that the **starting device** makes engine starts possible when climatic conditions would otherwise give rise to starting difficulties, the **idle speed circuit** permits no-load operation and the **main feed circuit** allows the attainment of all the performances that a car is expected to give under normal service conditions. Therefore, when the engine operates in the conditions illustrated in **A, Fig. 1, (no-load)**, only one of the three carburetors mentioned above is operative and yet is so self-sufficient that smooth operation is possible even without the contribution of the venturis, main jet, emulsion tube, etc.

With engine under **no-load (Fig. 1)** a gear engaged and the accelerator depressed, the **transition orifice** comes into play and progressively follows the engine **(diagram B)** until spray nozzle S takes over **(diagram C)**.

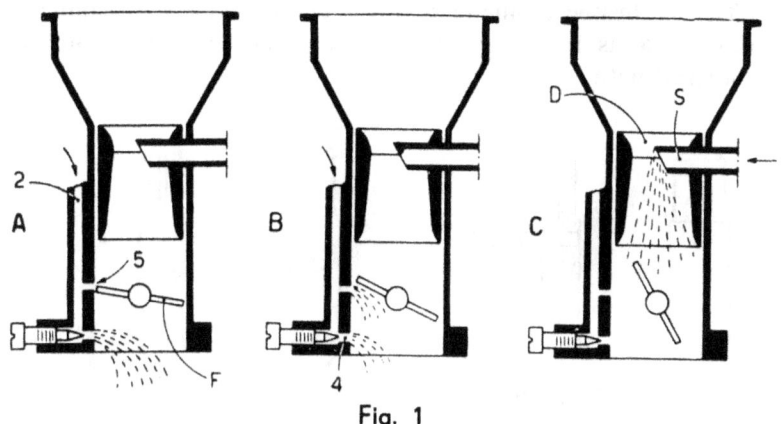

Fig. 1

D Venturi - F Throttle - S Spray nozzle -

2. Idle speed mixture duct - 4. Idle speed mixture orifice - 5. Transition orifice.

Each of the three small carburetors considered has a specifc task within well-defined limits: if one retards or advances its function engine operation will be irregular. This is why the tuning of a carburetor consists in synchronizing the three components.

IDLE SPEED AND PROGRESSION CIRCUIT

Considering that to obtain the desired smoothness of engine operation at idle speed and during progressive acceleration the supply of an air/fuel mixture of suitable strength is an essential condition, it follows that the carburetor must necessarily incorporate one calibrated jet—**idle speed jet**—to meter the fuel and another calibrated jet—**idle speed air jet**—to meter the air: the mixture thus preformed is quantitatively adjusted by an **idle speed mixture set screw** and will then be ready to blend with the air drawn in by the engine across the throttle opening.

Such an idle speed air jet may consist of a true jet or, much more usually, of a calibrated orifice, and has the purpose of correcting the fuel flow in the idle speed circuit. When we speak of varying the correction, we refer to an idle speed air orifice the diametric variation of which results in a change of fuel flow from the idle speed jet.

Two idle speed correction systems are adopted on WEBER carburetors:
a) - correcting action obtained in the idle speed jet itself;
b) - correcting action obtained in the carburetor body or by an independent air jet.

The calibrated diameter of these correction orifices must be considered as metering elements and, as such, must not be tampered with.

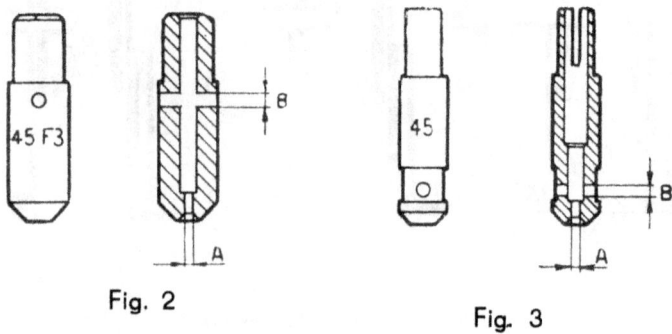

Fig. 2   Fig. 3

Figs. **2 and 3** show, respectively, an idle speed jet with incorporated correction **(system a** above) and an idle speed jet with independent correction **(system b** above). There is a further important element distinguishing the types of idle speed jets: for instance, the jet of **DR** type carburetors is stamped with the letter **F** meaning that the correction incorporated in the jet is in acordance with system **a** and, hence, the correction hole diameter, **(dimension B, Fig. 2)** is rigorously calibrated.

On the other hand, when no identification letter is found on the idle speed jet, the correction is obtained in the carburetor body. In this case **(dimension B, Fig. 3)** the hole, or holes, drilled in the jet are simply fuel passages.

Two examples of correction system designations are:
1) **45 F3** — system **a.**
2) **45**   — system **b.**

In both cases, number **45** indicates the jet's calibrated diameter **(in 1/100 of mm)** while symbol **F3** identifies the particular amount of correction which the jet in question incorporates. There are several types of correction design, each identified by its own symbol: a **45 F3** jet is **corrected** in a different way from a **45 F5** jet.

Symbols **F3, F5** etc., represent units of measure and are only indicative values. Dimension **A** (**Figs. 2 and 3**) both show the diameter of the jet.

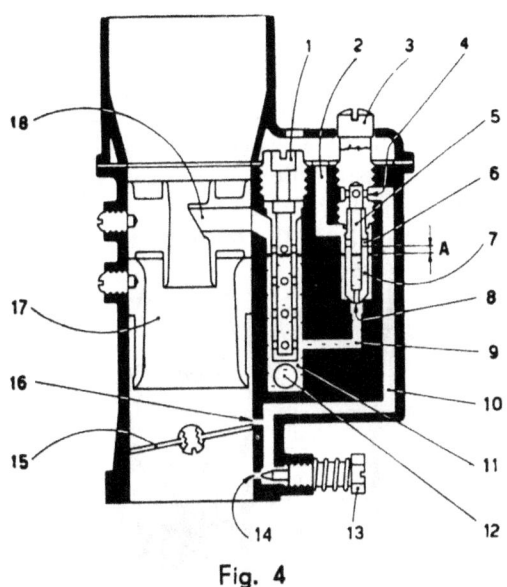

Fig. 4

1. Air corrector jet - **2**. Idle speed air duct - **3**. Idle speed jet holder - **4**. Mixture passage holes - **5**. Idle speed jet axial orifice - **6**. Calibrated correcting orifices - **7**. Idle speed jet - **8**. Calibrated orifice - **9**. Duct, idle speed jet-to-well - **10**. Idle speed mixture duct - **11**. Well - **12**. Duct, main jet-to-well - **13**. Idle speed mixture adjustment screw - **14**. Idle speed mixture orifice - **15**. Throttle **16**. Transition orifice - **17**. Primary Venturi - **18**. Spray nozzle.

Let us now consider the carburetor shown in **Fig. 4** where the type **a** correction system is obtained directly on idle speed jet **7** by two calibrated orifices **6**. Since the throttle is almost completely closed, the engine-promoted vacuum acts on idle speed orifice **14** whose adjustment is obtained by means of taper point screw **13**.

Through duct **10** the vacuum reaches mixture passage holes **4** and then, via the jet body, correction orifices **6** which are open to the atmosphere through duct **2**. The vacuum downstream of the throttle lifts the natural level of the fuel which, by overcoming head **A** is pre-emulsioned with the correction air and flows down to the engine after passing through duct **10** and receiving a quantitative metering by mixture adjustment screw **13**.

Orifice **8** represents the calibrated part of the jet and is a very important element because it meters the amount of fuel that blends with the air **metered** by correction orifices **6**.

In this design, from bowl **11** fuel reaches the idle speed jet through duct **9**.

The idle speed circuit correction obtained in carburetor body (system **b**) is seen in **Fig. 5** when an example of an **IM** series carburetor is shown.

In this case, only the indication of diameter calibration is stamped on idle speed jet **5**. Correction is obtained here by a specially designed and calibrated bush called **idle speed air bush** and marked **2** in the illustration.

Clearly visible in **Fig. 5** are the following:

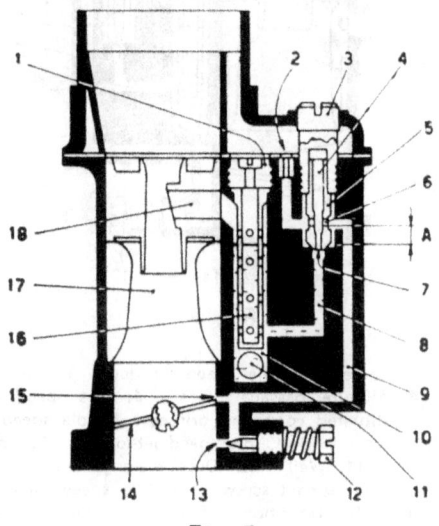

Fig. 5

1. Air corrector jet - **2**. Idle speed air bush - **3**. Idle speed jet holder - **4**. Idle speed jet axial hole - **5**. Idle speed jet - **6**. Idle speed mixture transfer holes 7. Metering orifice - **8**. Duct, well-to-idle speed jet - **9**. Idle speed mixture duct - **10**. Well - **11**. Duct, main jet-to-well - **12**. Idle speed mixture set screw - **13**. Idle speed orifice - **14**. Throttle - **15**. Transition orifice - **16**. Emulsion tube - **17**. Primary Venturi - **18**. Spray nozzle.

A — Idle speed head
2 — Idle speed bush
3 — Idle speed jet holder
5 — Idle speed jet
6 — Idle speed mixture transfer holes
7 — Idle speed jet metering orifice
8 — Duct, well-to-idle speed jet
9 — Idle speed mixture duct

11 — Duct, main jet-to-well
16 — Emulsion tube (*).

(*) In common usage the emulsion tube is often called "emulsion well." This is an error because by "well" is intended the cavity where the emulsion tube is housed.

By overcoming head **A** the air drawn in through bush 2 lifts the fuel by the amount allowed by the calibration of orifice 7 under the idle speed jet 5.

Let us reconsider the vacuum that develops around idle speed orifice 13 when throttle 14 is almost totally closed: under these conditions the engine runs without load and supplies the bare power required to overcome the passive resistance of mechanical components. On account of the succession of intake stages, engine suction determines a pulsating air flow: the larger the number of cylinders the less pulsating will this suction be. It follows that in the purely theoretical case of an infinite number of cylinders, air would be aspirated steadily, without pulsations.

When the throttle is in the idle speed position, which is obtained by a set screw, the aspiration-promoted air flow finds its way across the gap around the throttle (**Fig. 6**).

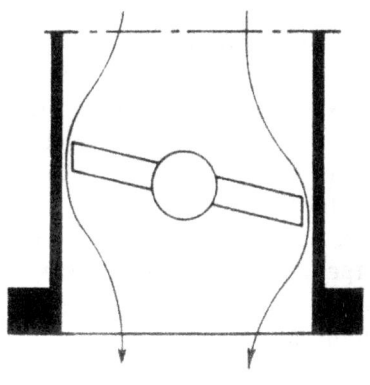

Fig. 6

It is this very gap that determines the degree of vacuum which, by acting on the idle speed orifice, draws out the air/fuel mixture required by the engine.

The idle speed orifice in the carburetor barrel is always located down-stream of the throttle while the transition orifice is always upstream.

With engine rpm steady, the greater the amount of throttle closing the stronger the vacuum on idle speed orifice in the inlet duct; due account being taken of the fact that beyond a given throttle choking limit the engine cannot keep going.

Idle speed adjustment: if we pose ourselves the problem of determining the **sensitivity** of idle speed adjustment in an engine running under no-load and with idle speed mixture set screw perfectly adjusted: we must then turn the set screw and find out by how many degrees it must be rotated, either way, before engine rpm drops as a result of the **leanness** or **richness** of the mixture.

Let us assume that after moving set screw **12** (**Fig. 5**) a quarter turn the engine rpm drops and that the same thing happens when the screw is turned the same amount the other way; in this case the screw has a **sensitivity** of a ½ turn (¼ + ¼). If it is desired to increase this sensitivity, just widen the idle speed orifice, say, from 110 to 120.

Under these conditions, in fact, by acting on screw **12** the **annular** gap around its taper point is wider than the original one. We thus notice that the sensitivity of screw **12** is no longer of half a turn (180°) but less (for instance, 130°).

We shall now consider the condition in which an idle speed circuit may be defined as properly adjusted. For normal automotive engines the idle speed rate is generally in the 450-600 rpm range.

Assuming we have an engine whose rotational speed is within acceptable limits, the following considerations may be made:

1) By turning in the mixture set screw, the engine rpm increases: in this case, the mixture is **rich** and the screw must be closed until the point of maximum angular speed is reached, without modifying the throttle opening.

2) By turning out the mixture set screw, the engine rpm increases: this time the mixture is **lean** and the action to be taken is exactly the opposite to 1), the mixture must be strengthened to obtain the optimum ratio.

3) By turning either in or out the mixture set screw, the engine rpm decreases: carburetion is now the best possible, i.e., the mixture set screw is in the right position to supply the desirable air/fuel mixture.

As a rule, once the optimum set screw position is found it is advisable to leave the screw just a bit open, that is, slightly on the **rich** side.

In attempting to define what is exactly meant by a proper idle speed adjustment we may say that it is the setting which allows engine operation at the maximum rpm rate with respect to a given throttle opening.

Transition or (progression) orifice.

As explained previously, the vacuum around the idle speed mixture orifice in the carburetor barrel **(Fig. 1)** is strongest when the engine is running under no-load but when the accelerator pedal is pressed this vacuum decreases: as a result, less mixture is supplied while more air is drawn in by the engine. The mixture becomes excessively weak and the progression of engine acceleration is faulty.

Hence, an additional supply of mixture must necessarily be contributed to compensate for this idle speed orifice deficiency and allow the engine to pick up speed. To this end, a hole called the **transition orifice** is drilled in the barrel, in line with the upper edge of the throttle, so that it will be uncovered as soon as the throttle is acted upon and will thus be in a condition to supply its mixture.

As a calibrated metering element, the transition orifice is incorporated in every carburetor; even **2** or **3** of these orifices may be present, however, depending on functional requirements. Their diameter is dependent upon engine characteristics and their location is always referred to the throttle in its fully-closed position. The transition orifice(s) is upstream of the throttle and dimension **B**, **(Fig. 7)**, represents the orifice **blanking head**, namely, the distance which the lower edge of throttle must travel before the orifice can supply any mixture.

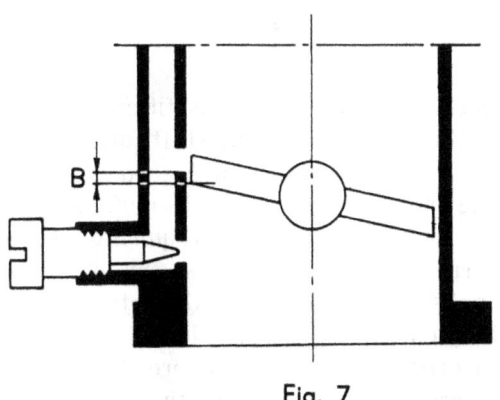

Fig. 7

This head and the diameter of the orifice are two factors of primary importance. While the diameter has great significance from the functional standpoint, dimension **B** determines the instant in which the transition orifice begins to supply the mixture.

In fact, as long as head **B** is not **completely overcome** the vacuum on the transition orifice will not be strong enough to force out the mixture and the engine will be fed by the idle speed orifice alone.

Thus, if head **B** is changed, also the progression range of acceleration will vary; this is the reason why the transition orifice is always drilled in reference to the throttle.
It should be noted that with respect to the carburetor barrel longitudinal axis (**Fig. 8**), the fully-closed throttle forms a given angle: this angle is marked on all throttles and is a determining factor which, if varied, will also change head **B**.

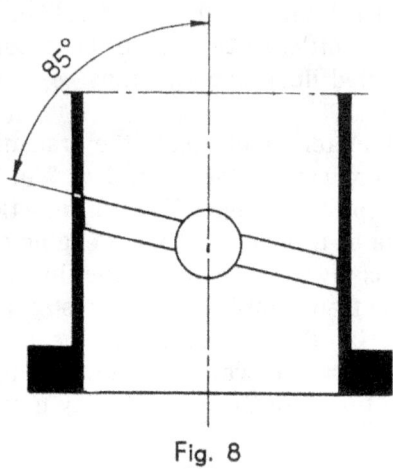

Fig. 8

For instance, if an 87° throttle is fitted in place of an 85° throttle, head **B** is inevitably changed. It follows, evidently, that when a replacement is made the new throttle must necessarily have the same inclination (marked in degrees) as the one replaced. In case of a major overhaul requiring a polishing of the carburetor barrel, remember that also this operation may vary the head: if polishing increases the diameter of the barrel, evidently the fully-closed throttle would be located farther from the transition orifice than it was before. Let us now see what functional consequences arise from the erroneous position of head **B**. In **Fig. 9** the throttle is **always in the same idle speed position** but, according to the position of transition orifice we, have:
diagram A—correct location of orifice and head
diagram B—orifice moved upstream: positive head
diagram C—orifice moved downstream: negative head.

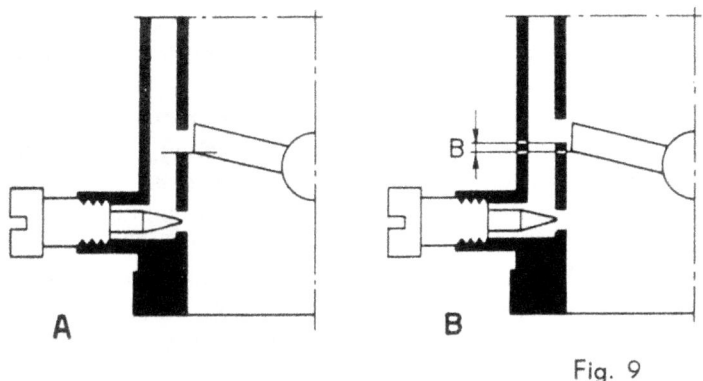

Fig. 9

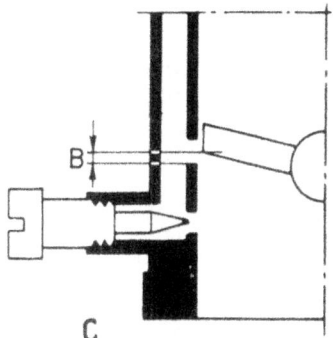

Correct location of orifice and head—Diagram A.
Idle speed operation and progressive acceleration are normal. When engine idles, the transition orifice is excluded since it is not yet uncovered but simply tangent to throttle.

Orifice moved upstream: positive head—Diagram B.
Idle speed operation is normal but in the progressive acceleration stage a **flat spot** develops and the engine may stop because of excessive mixture leanness.

In fact, being too high upstream, the transition orifice is acted upon by the vacuum a bit too late: consequently, the mixture leans out because the engine promotes a flow of air which is excessive in relation to the amount of fuel supplied by the idle speed orifice in the carburetor barrel.

Orifice below throttle: negative head—Diagram C.
Irregular running is generally due to a rich mixture. In fact,

owing to the negative value of the head the transition orifice is under vacuum also at idle speed and, therefore, delivers fuel which enriches the mixture.

Under these conditions, cases are met in which the engine runs at idling speed with completely tightened, idle adjustment screw, galloping engines, etc. Again, referring to **diagrams A and B, Fig. 9**, it may be said that in both cases idling is normal, but if the situation is examined more closely it will be seen that in **diagram B** the adjusting screw is more open than in **diagram A**, so that, when the engine is in the suction stroke, some of the air enters the mixture duct above the throttle and leans he preformed mixture.

In the discussion on **Fig. 9** we analized the engine operation to find out the irregularities. Let us now see how the defects may be remedied in practice.

In the case of **diagram A of Fig. 9** everything is regular and no action need be taken.

For **diagram B,** on the other hand, the head must be corrected to the required value and this is obtained by machining a small chamfer in the throttle (**Fig. 10**) so that the excessive head is

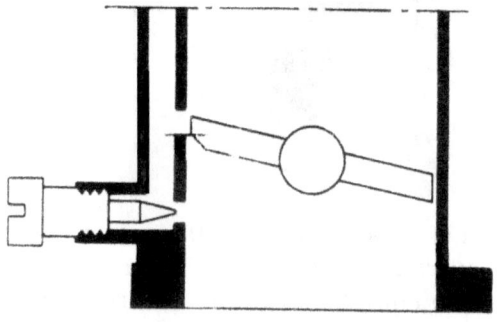

Fig. 10

reduced. This operation must be performed in steps, by trial. The condition shown in **diagram C of Fig. 9** is corrected by drilling a small hole in the throttle on the side opposite the idle orifice (**Fig. 11**): some of the air drawn in by the engine may then flow through this hole and thus the throttle may remain more closed.

Enlarge the hole by small increments until the throttle blanks entirely the transition orifice thus providing the required head.

It is understood that the above remedies—i.e., chamfer and hole—are to be considered as actions taken to correct only **small carburetion troubles** arising from replacement of the throttle, cleaning of the barrel, etc.

So, for instance, in the case of **Fig. 11** it is of no use trying to increase the head once the throttle has reached the closed position because of the hole drilled in it.

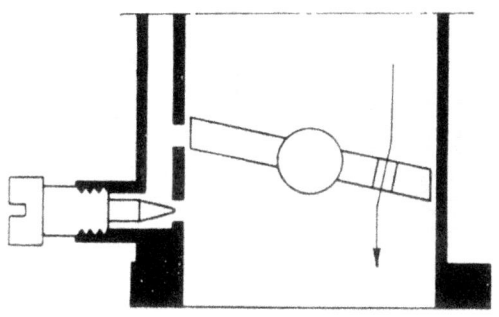

Fig. 11

It now remains to be seen how a correct carburetion in the progression range may be checked.

Theoretically, once the idle speed is properly adjusted, the position of the mixture adjusting screw should remain unchanged throughout the progression range.

In practice, however, things may be different and the progression could be either so slightly on the rich or lean side that under a normal inspection, carburetion appears correct.

After adjusting the idle speed, turn the throttle opening setscrew so as to increase the engine RPM rate (e.g., from 500 to 800 RPM) but not up to the point where the nozzle starts operating. After this, check if at this speed (800 RPM) the mixture screw may still be left in the pre-established position.

For example: if by further backing the idle mixture adjustment screw at 800 RPM the engine speeds up, this means that the progression mixture is lean. On the other hand, if the engine speeds up when the screw is turned in the mixture is rich.

In the no-load operation it is advisable to adjust the mixture screw so as to render less marked the progression defect, even if idling smoothness must be partially sacrificed.

In the following figures some examples of solutions adopted for idle mixture duct drilling are given.

Fig. 4 shows a classic diagram where the idle speed jet is supplied with fuel by well **11** which, in turn, receives fuel from the bowl through the main jet and duct **12**.

This is the more common arrangement, but in some designs the idle jet receives fuel directly from the bowl.

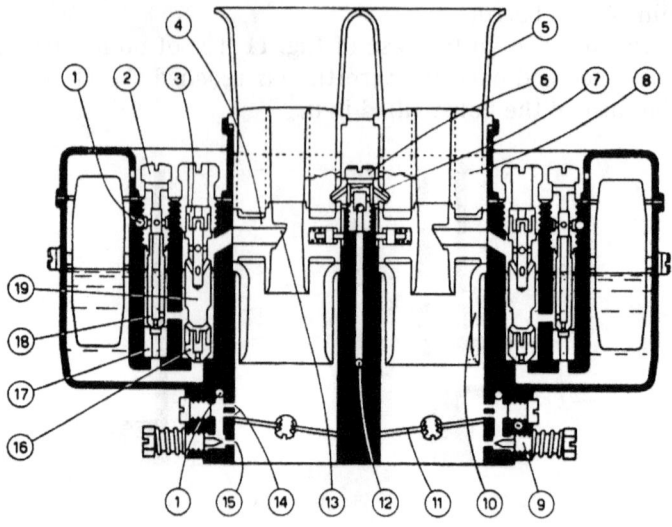

Fig. 12

An intermediate solution is illustrated in **Fig. 12** where the idle speed fuel is derived both from the bowl (back of main jet) and from the well. This last arrangement is common with the **40 IF-4C** carburetors for Aston-Martin, Pegaso Z102, Ferrari 166-250-375 engines, etc.

As to the idle mixture circuit of **Fig. 13** in which fuel is drawn from the well, it should be noted how the fuel delivery duct is generally on a level with the last row of air corrector holes in the emulsion tube.

The position of the duct is justified by the fact that when the engine runs at full speed duct **13** too is empty, but as soon as the accelerator is released the engine would tend to stop if the idle speed jet were not immediately supplied with fuel from the well.

By deriving duct **13** at the height of the last row of the air corrector holes in the emulsion tube the above duct is more promptly filled with fuel resulting in improved acceleration progression when the engine is subjected to quick and successive accelerations.

MAIN FEED SYSTEM

This second section will deal in detail with the following items.
a) main jet
b) main jet holder
c) emulsion tube
d) air corrector jet

e) venturi (primary)
f) venturi (auxiliary) and nozzle
g) constant-level system

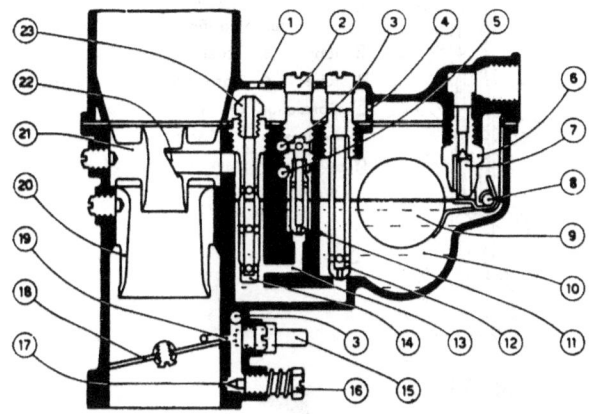

Fig. 13

1. Air inlet port - 2. Idle speed jet holder - 3. Idle mixture duct - 4. Bowl air orifice - 5. Idle air duct - 6. Needle valve - 7. Valve needle - 8. Float fulcrum pin - 9. Float - 10. Bowl - 11. Idle speed jet - 12. Main jet - 13. Duct, idle speed jet to well - 14. Emulsion tube - 15. Vacuum advance connection tube - 16. Idle mixture adjustment screw - 17. Idle speed orifice to throat - 18. Throttle - 19. Transition orifice - 20. Primary Venturi - 21. Auxiliary Venturi - 22 Nozzle - 23. Air corrector jet.

The first step is to investigate how mixture is formed in the well. For reference see **Fig.** 14 showing a section of downdraft carburetor **DR**.

The fuel flows from the bowl, through duct **10**, to well **11** where it reaches the same level as in the bowl.

Until no vacuum acts on nozzle **1** the fuel level in the well is as indicated by measure **A**.

As soon as the vacuum created by engine suction acts on nozzle **1**, air enters through air corrector orifice **2**, is metered by calibrated hole **3**, flows through axial hole **5** of emulsion tube **4** and issues through calibrated holes **6**. In its high-speed flow the air drags along fuel by overcoming the liquid head **B** and the emulsion thus formed reches nozzle **1** where it mixes with the air stream flowing through the throat.

As the engine speed increases, a larger amount of air flows through corrector orifice **2**, and progressive uncovering of holes **7**, **8** and **9** occurs until space **5** remains empty and the fuel level drops down to the height of the last row of emulsion holes.

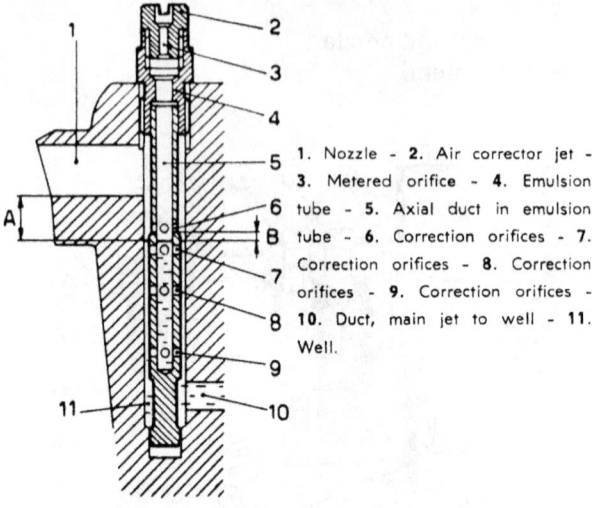

Fig. 14

1. Nozzle - 2. Air corrector jet - 3. Metered orifice - 4. Emulsion tube - 5. Axial duct in emulsion tube - 6. Correction orifices - 7. Correction orifices - 8. Correction orifices - 9. Correction orifices - 10. Duct, main jet to well - 11. Well.

When the engine is slowed down the decrease in vacuum causes a progressive rise of fuel in the well until at idling speed its level again reaches the height of fuel in the bowl.

In the following analysis of the elements forming the main feed system the importance of every item in regard to its specific function will become apparent.

Main jet

This jet is the calibrated part that is most sensitive to possible tampering. **Fig. 15** shows a standard jet housed in its holder; radial holes C are transfer-orifices.

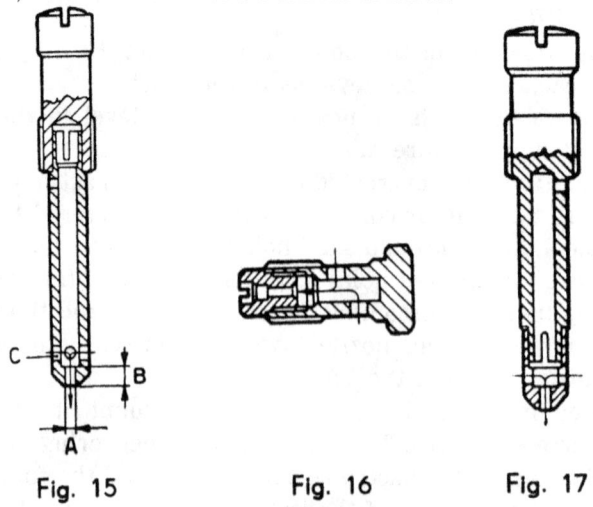

Fig. 15   Fig. 16   Fig. 17

16

By observing the jet it is seen that its capacity depends on dimensions **A** and **B**.

It is apparent that, considering two jets, identical in diameter (dimension **A**), but differing in the length of the calibrated portion, the shorter jet in **B** will have a greater capacity.

In fact, in this case load losses will be lesser and a greater amount of fuel issues through the jet.

All jets used in Weber Carburetors are stamped with diameter dimension **A** (**in hundredths of millimeter**). As regards actual operation, the diameter of the four transfer holes **C** will be such as to warrant, in any case, a capacity greater than rated. **Fig. 16 and 17** illustrate two other types of main jets mounted in their holders.

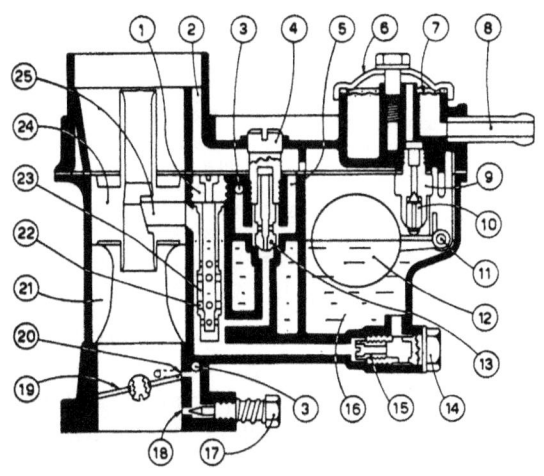

Fig. 18

1. Air corrector jet - **2.** Air inlet duct - **3.** Idle mixture duct - **4.** Idle jet holder - **5.** Idle air duct - **6.** Filter cover - **7.** Filter gauze · **8.** Fuel inlet connection - **9.** Needle valve - **10.** Valve needle - **11.** Float fulcrum pin - **12.** Float - **13.** Idle speed jet - **14.** Main jet holder - **15.** Main jet - **16.** Fuel bowl - **17.** Idle mixture adjustment screw - **18.** Orifice, idle orifice to throat - **19.** Throttle - **20.** Transition orifice - **21.** Primary Venturi - **22.** Emulsion orifices - **23.** Emulsion tube - **24.** Auxiliary Venturi - **25.** Spray nozzle.

The application of main jet **15** and of jet **14** is shown in **Figs. 18 and 19** respectively. The jet in **Fig. 15** is bayonet-coupled directly to the holder while that in **Fig. 17** is held in place by the holder tip bayonet-coupled to holder body. The jet in **Fig. 16**, instead, is screwed tightly into the holder.

The jets are accurately checked with very sensitive air flowmeters and the accuracy of machining allows perfect inter-

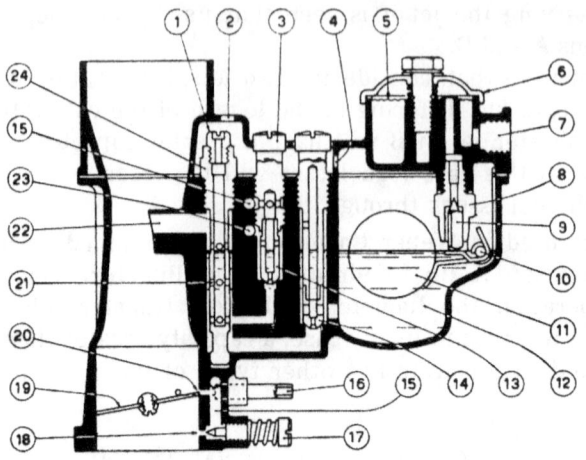

Fig. 19

1. Air corrector jet - 2. Air inlet port - 3. Idle jet holder - 4. Bowl air port - 5. Filter gauze - 6. Filter cover - 7. Fuel inlet connection - 8. Needle valve - 9. Valve needle - 10. Float fulcrum pin - 11. Float - 12. Fuel bowl - 13. Idle speed jet - 14. Main jet - 15. Idle mixture duct -- 16. Vacuum advance connection - 17. Idle mixture adjusting screw - 18. Orifice, idle jet to duct - 19. Throttle - 20. Transition orifice - 21. Emulsion holes - 22. Nozzle - 23. Idle air duct - 24. Emulsion tube.

changeability. Should it be required to vary the capacity for functional resons, the jet must be replaced by another having a different calibration.

Entry of fuel into the calibrated portion of the jet may take place either upwards **(Figs. 15 and 17)** or downwards **(Figs. 20 and 21)**.

These figures show how emulsion tube 4 carries jet 7 at one end and air corrector 3 at the other.

Two main jets are installed in dual throat carburetors: each jet supplies one of the throats with fuel drawn from the bowl.

A dual throat carburetor may, therefore, be defective due to improper functioning of only one of the jets and this will cause irregular running of the engine.

Main jet holder

Some of the principal Weber-manufactured main jet holders are illustrated in the following figures:

Fig. 15—This jet holder is threaded on the outside to fit in the carburetor and carries an inner hole for jet mounting.

Fig. 16—This holder is mounted horizontally and is provided with two transversal holes on offset axes for better entrance of the incoming fuel from the bowl.

Fig. 20—Type of jet used on **OTS** carburetors. Compared with the others, it is particular in that it has two orifices for the admission of air to the corrector jet. Orifices 2 are not calibrated.

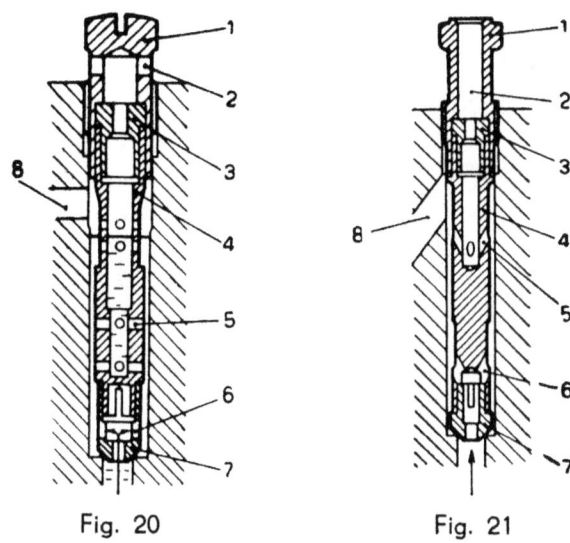

Fig. 20   Fig. 21

1. Emulsion tube holder - 2. Air holes - 3. Air corrector jet - 4. Emulsion tube - 5. Air corrector holes - 6. Fuel holes - 7. Main jet - 8. Mixture duct to nozzle.

1. Emulsion tube holder - 2. Air axial hole - 3. - Air corrector jet - 4. Emulsion tube - 5. Air corrector holes - 6. Fuel holes - 7. Main jet - 8. Mixture duct to nozzle.

Fig. 21—Type of jet used on special carburetors. Orifice 2 permits the entrance of air to the corrector jet and, contrary to the jet in **Fig. 20**, is drilled axially.

Emulsion tube

Its task is to emulsify the air previously metered by the corrector with the fuel coming from the main jet.

Fig. 22 shows the same emulsion tube illustrated in **Fig. 13** which is designed for the **DR** type carburetor.

The dimension diagram illustrated in **Fig. 22** is practically the same for all types of carburetors and may be taken as a basis for our study.

Dimensions G - H - I: are the diameters of the air corrector holes and are those which determine the acceleration progression regularity. Particularly important is diameter **G** of the first row of holes since it is the size of these holes, along with head **L**,

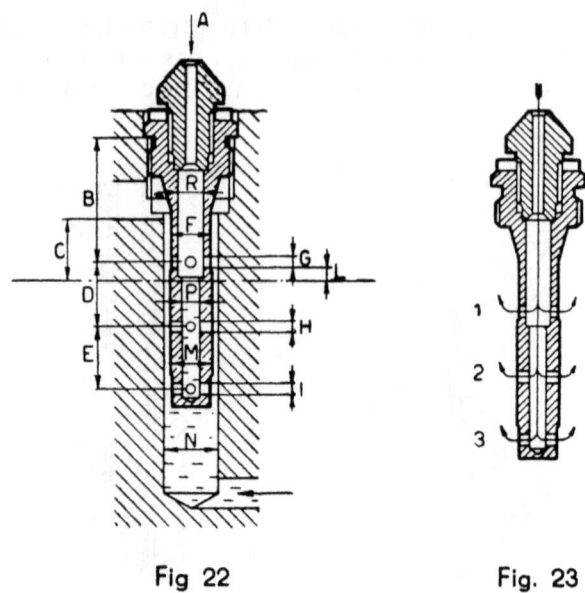

Fig 22   Fig. 23

that governs the beginning of delivery from the nozzle. If dimension **L** is less than specified the nozzle will start delivering fuel before time thus giving a rich mixture. Conversely, a lean mixture will result if **L** is in excess of the specified value.

It is therefore evident that head **L** has been so set as to be overcome only by a given vacuum at the nozzle. If the head is overcome before or after the specified vacuum at the nozzle is reached, acceleration irregularities will occur as described above. In fact, when at a given opening of the throttle both the idle jet and the transition orifice are not sufficiently responsive to the vacuum formed in the throat, the engine must be fed by the nozzle. But, for instance, if **L** is excessive, with the throttle opened as indicated above, the vacuum at the nozzle will still not be such as to cause fuel to issue from the nozzle and therefore a lean mixture will be had in the acceleration stage.

Dimensions M - N: diameter **M** is the true dimension of the emulsion tube. In fact, the same carburetor body will adapt emulsion tubes with different diameters **M** though well diameter **N** remains the same. **Fig. 23** illustrates the air flow path in the emulsion tube during full-throttle running.

Figs. 24-25 and 26 illustrate some emulsion tubes for Weber carburetors.

It should be noted that the tubes shown in **Fig. 26** are not

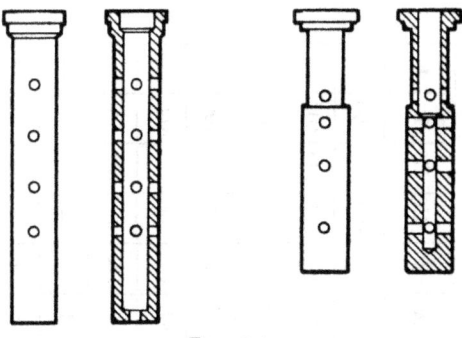

Fig. 26

thread-mounted but are fitted free in the carburetor body: they are kept in place by the air corrector jet when it is screwed into place.

Furthermore, it is again pointed out that every emulsion tube is stamped with a symbol that identifies it from the others which, though having the same serial number, have different dimensions.

The chart of **Fig. 27** shows that among emulsion tube metered parts identified by letters **A-B-C-D-E-F**, both diameter **A** and the diameter of the air corrector holes may vary. The result is that the emulsion tube identified as **TS 534a** takes the suffix **F.6 - F.10 - F.15 depending on the diameter of the air corrector holes.** An emulsion tube may be fully identified only if the Serial Number is followed by the size of the corrector holes, the latter also being the corrector system symbol.

Air corrector jet

This jet meters the amount of air that enters the emulsion tube and mixes with the fuel. It is a metered part having the same importance as the main jet with the exception that functions are reversed: when the corrector jet diameter is increased the mixture is weaker.

In **Figs. 14, 21, 22 and 28** different types of air corrector jets are shown.

As for the main jets, so also the corrector jets have a working capacity which varies with metered diameter and the length of the calibrated portion. The number stamped on the jets indicates the diameter expressed in hundredths of a millimeter.

Primary venturi

The vacuum created by the cylinders draws air from outside.

Tube type	A	B	C	D	E	F
F 4	5^{25}	125	100	—	100	—
F 5	6^{25}	125	100	125	100	—
F 6	5^{25}	125	100	—	100	125
F 8	5^{25}	125	100	125	100	125
F 9	6^{25}	125	100	125	100	125
F 10	4	125	95	125	95	—
F 11	4	—	—	125	95	—
F 15	6	200	—	—	—	—

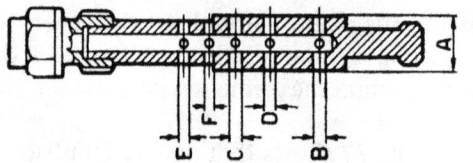

Fig. 27

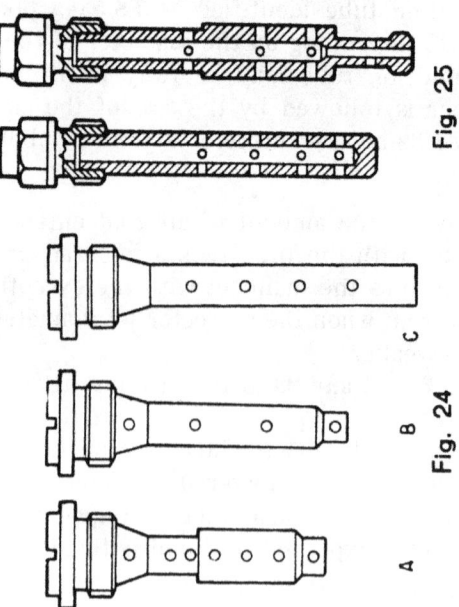

Fig. 25

Fig. 24

This air, after passing through the carburetor air clener, reaches the carburetor air horn and then the throat. Due to the restriction provided by the venturi the air speed is increased and a vacuum is formed which draws fuel from the nozzle. The greater the restriction of the venturi the greter the vacuum at the nozzle which, therefore, will draw a greater amount of fuel from the well.

However, no variation in the venturi constriction is possible in any venturi since this variation calls for replacement of the main jet; because in a properly designed carburetor these two parts are correlated.

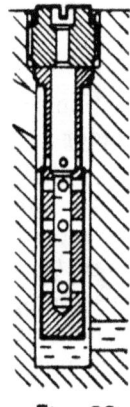

Fig. 28

Operating conditions may be as follows:
A) by reducing the venturi—and consequently the main jet—power and consumption will drop but pick up will remain good;
B) by increasing the venturi alone consumption will drop but pick up will be worsened;
C) by increasing both venturi and main jet, power and consumption increase. Pick up is less brilliant but the drawback is easily overcome by installing an accelerating pump.

The possible increase in power is, of course, dependent on engine characteristics.

Stamped on every venturi is a number corresponding to its diameter, expressed in millimeters.

Auxiliary venturi

The auxiliary venturi (**Fig. 29**) carries calibrated nozzle S which communicates with the well.

Engine suction will create a vacuum at the nozzle varying with the throttle opening, engine RPM and the diameter of the

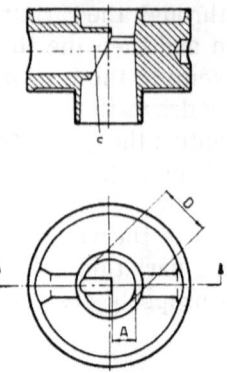

Fig. 29

primary venturi. The nozzle section has a considerable bearing on fuel consumption. The diameter of the nozzle is stamped on every auxiliary venturi in mm., e.g., 3 - 3.5 - 4 - 4.5, etc. The auxiliary venturi rarely undergoes damage liable to impair its functional efficiency. However, care must be taken during assembly to prevent deformations that might possibly alter dimensions **D** and **A**. In fact, if these dimensions are reduced the vacuum at the nozzle increases and consumption would increase. Also a flattening of the nozzle would affect consumption.

Constant-level system
The fuel level in a bowl may reach different heights depending on the adjustment of the tang supporting needle valve **10 (Fig. 18)**.

Once a given setting has been established and a given type of carburetor decided, the fuel level in the bowl becomes one of the factors determining the adjustment. In fact, it is the level in the bowl that establishes the **head** of fuel.

To prevent changes in level, and therefore in the head, the carburetor is so designed that the level is kept steady even when the liquid mass in the bowl is subjected to dynamic stresses as occurs on curves and under acceleration and deceleration conditions. Special provisions are made for both the float and the bowl when the carburetor may be subject to operating on steep slopes, as in the case of the agricultural tractor carburetor in **Fig. 30**.

In any case the carburetor installation must be such that the bowl is oriented in the direction of forward travel.

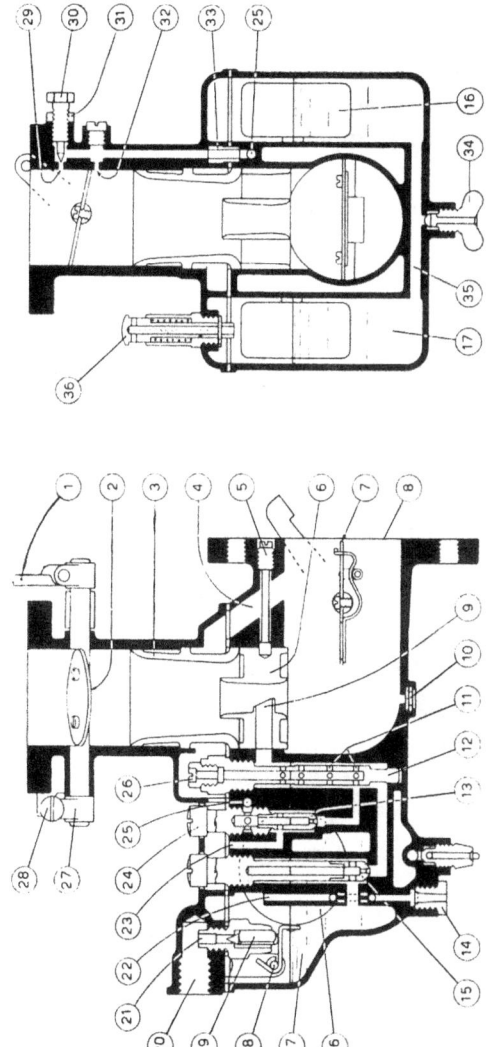

Fig. 30

1. Primary throttle control lever - **2.** Primary throttle - **3.** Primary Venturi - **4.** Air corrector intake duct - **5.** Auxiliary Venturi fixing screw - **6.** Auxiliary Venturi - **7.** Starting throttle - **8.** Air horn - **9.** Main nozzle - **10.** Air horn drain plug - **11.** Emulsion holes - **12.** Emulsion tube - **13.** Idle speed jet - **14.** Bowl air duct plug - **15.** Main jet - **16.** Float - **17.** Bowl - **18.** Float fulcrum pin - **19.** Valve needle - **20.** Fuel inlet connection - **21.** Needle valve - **22.** Bowl air duct - **23.** Idle speed air duct - **24.** Idle speed jet holder - **25.** Idle mixture duct - **26.** Air corrector jet - **27.** Sector for primary throttle - **28.** Idle speed adjustment screw - **29.** Orifice, idle jet to duct - **30.** Idle mixture adjustment screw - **31.** Locknut - **32.** Transition orifice - **33.** Idle mixture duct bush - **34.** Bowl drain cock - **35.** Bowl drain duct - **36.** Primer rod.

STARTING DEVICE (STARTER)

The starting systems are based on two principles:
1) Auxiliary carburetor system
2) Choke system

They may be actuated manually, i.e., directly by the driver, or operate automatically under the action of a thermo-sensitive control (bi-metallic lamina or thermostatic capsule).

Auxiliary carburetor systems

They consist of a small carburetor incorporated in the main carburetor and may be of three types:

a) plain valve
b) Economy-Super-Aspiration (E.S.A.) device
c) progressive operation

Type a) includes the starting valve devices which, by a manual control, may be thrown in or out without intermediate settings.

Type b) covers the devices which, besides the above fixed positions, permit intermediate settings either for economic running or over-feeding.

The devices which supply the engine with a mixture whose composition and amount are variable, depending on the extent of insertion of the device itself, belong to type c).

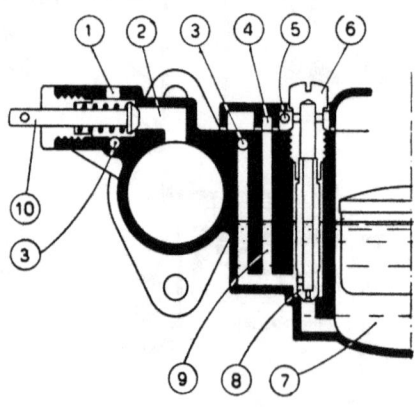

Fig. 31

1. Emulsion air orifice - **2.** Starting mixture duct - **3.** Starting mixture duct - **4.** Emulsion air slot - **5.** Emulsion air orifice - **6.** Starting jet holder - **7.** Bowl - **8.** Starting jet - **9.** Reserve starting well - **10.** Starting valve.

Plain valve starting device

Fig. 31 illustrates the **OTS** type of carburetor starting device. The fuel, coming directly from bowl **7**, flows through metered jet **8** and reaches the same height as in the bowl. With the throttle in the idle position and taper valve **10** being open, the vacuum promoted by the starter-cranked engine acts on duct **3** and draws the mixture already blended with air coming through orifice **5**. Still under the action of vacuum, air enters through orifice **1** and blends with the mixture pre-formed in duct **3**.

Fig. 32 shows the diagram of the **DCLD** dual-throat carburetor starting device. A two-position climatic control is fitted in this case (**E** = **Summer; I** = **Winter**) so as to have available two grades of mixture depending on climatic conditions. If control **6** is turned with the letter **I** in line with index **12** the mixture will be richer. Conversely, mixture will be leaner when letter **E** is lined up with index **12**.

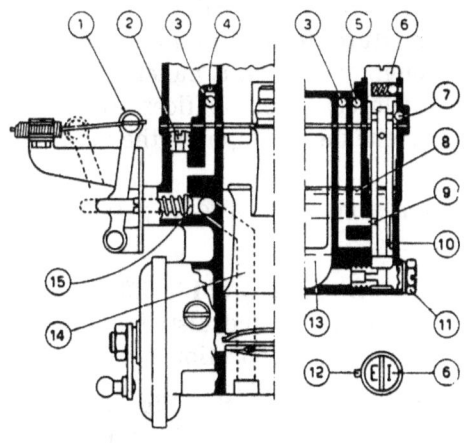

Fig. 32

1. Starting valve control lever - 2. Starting air jet - 3. Mixture duct - 4. Emulsion air orifice - 5. Emulsion air orifice - 6. Starting mixture control - 7. Air control orifice - 8. Reserve starting well - 9. Climatic control orifice (summer) - 10. Climatic control orifice (winter) - 11. Starting jet - 12. Starting mixture adjustment screw index - 13. Bowl - 14. Starting mixture duct - 15. Starting valve.

By considering the position of **Fig. 32 (summer)** it may be seen how the fuel passes from bowl **13** to metered jet **11**. As valve **15** is opened—the throttles being in th idle speed position —the engine-promoted vacuum draws, through duct **3**, the mixture formed by fuel arriving from starting jet **11** and air through orifices **5** and **7**. Since the control is in the **E (summer)** position, the mixture flows through calibrated hole **9**. Were the control to be oriented on **I (winter)** the mixture would pass through hole **10** whose diameter is larger than that of hole **9**.

Economy-Super-Aspiration(E.S.A.)

The E.S.A. is mounted in two versions (carburetors of the

DR and DRN series) illustrated respectively in **Figs. 33** and **34**. These versions are similar, with the exception that in the **DR** type carburetor the supplementary air inlet is provided through a rack-controlled valve while, in the **DRN** type carburetor the air inlet is provided through the rotation of a movable diaphragm.

From the operational diagram in **Fig. 33** it is apparent that fuel arrives from the bowl through duct **8**, passes metered E.S.A. jet **7**, orifice **1** (summer) or **3** (winter) of climatic control **2**, valve **9**, E.S.A. valve **10**, duct **11** and finally flows to the throat downstream of the throttle.

For a correct and proper operation of the E.S.A. the letter stamped on climatic control **2** (**E** = **summer; I** = **winter**) must correspond with the reference index on the carburetor cover. In this way the mixture, formed by fuel coming from jet **7** and air drawn in through orifices **4**, is metered by calibrated orifice **1 (summer)** or **3 (winter)**. These orifices are drilled in control **2** in such a way that the device supplies the most suitable mixture ratio.

E.S.A. operation under the several possible conditions is as follows:

Normal operation — Diagram A of Fig. 33

The E.S.A. taper valve **10** and distributor **12** are closed: the device is inoperative and carburetion normal.

Economic operation — Diagram B of Fig. 33

By partially pulling the knob on the panel, without overcoming the stiffening point determined by the spring dog, the bowden-controlled lever **13** causes the rotation of gear **16** which lifts rack **15** and, hence, distributor **12** from its seat. Taper valve **10** is kept shut by a spring housed in the rack.

This causes a supplementary passage of air coming from the carburetor horn through duct **14** ending in the carburetor throat, downstream of the primary venturi.

By-passing the primary and the auxiliary venturis the air does not promote the suction of fuel from the nozzle and consequently the mixture is weakened thus permitting a reduced fuel consumption.

Starting or overfeeding operation — Diagram C of Fig. 33

By pulling the knob on the panel fully over, gear **16** rotates a further angle and completely lifts rack **15** which, in turn, raises taper valve **10** from its seat. under these conditions and with throttle in idle position the vacuum promoted by the

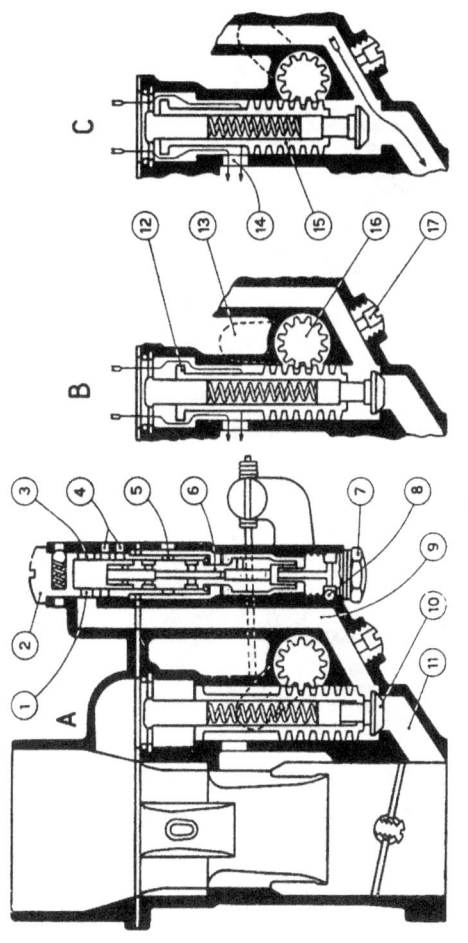

Fig. 33

1. Mixture orifice (summer) - 2. E.S.A. control - 3. Mixture orifice (winter) - 4. Emulsion air holes - 5. Supplementary air hole - 6. Sliding tube - 7. E.S.A. jet - 8. Fuel duct - 9. Mixture duct - 10. E.S.A. valve - 11. E.S.A. mixture duct - 12. Distributor - 13. E.S.A. control lever - 14. Supplementary air duct - 15. Rack - 16. Gear - 17. E.S.A. air jet.

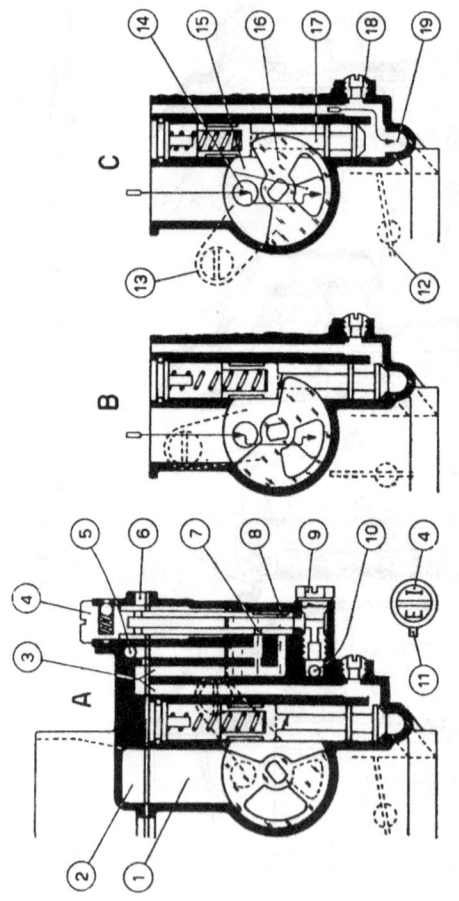

Fig. 34

1. Supplementary air duct - 2. Supplementary air intake - 3. Mixture ducts - 4. E.S.A. control - 5. Emulsion air orifice - 6. Emulsion air orifice - 7. Mixture orifice (summer) - 8. Mixture orifice (winter) - 9. E.S.A. jet - 10. Fuel duct - 11. E.S.A. control index - 12. Throttle - 13. E.S.A. control lever - 14. Supplementary air comunication slots - 15. Fixed diaphragm - 16. Movable diaphragm - 17. E.S.A. valve - 18. E.S.A. air jet - 19. Mixture duct.

starter-cranked engine causes the fuel to be first emulsified with air entering through orifices 4. The mixture thus formed flows in duct 9, reaches taper valve 10 and is finally emulsified with the air drawn in through the hole metered by screw 17 and is conveyed to the carburetor throat downstream of the throttle via duct 11. With the engine started the engine-promoted vacuum on sliding tube 6 increases and tube 6 rises and uncovers supplementary inlet port 5 through which emulsifying air is admitted with the consequent leaning out of the mixture drawn in through the E.S.A. This ensures a correct mixture even during the period in which the starting device operates. In this same starting position, **but with wide-open throttle**, the E.S.A. may also serve as **overfeeder** because, by permitting the entrance of an additional amount of mixture and air drawn in respectively through duct 14 and 11 it boosts engine power by supplying a richer mixture.

How to use the E.S.A.

The rules to follow in order to derive the best advantages offered by the E.S.A. are briefly outlined below:

Normal operation (Diagram A of Fig. 33)—Knob at rest against panel: normal carburetion.

Economic operation (Diagram B of Fig. 33)—**Knob in intermediate position**: as set by the spring loaded dog: to be used with engine well warmed up, on lovel roads, also with partial and variable throttle openings. In this position the device may serve also as an altitude corrector on mountain journeys, above 2000 meters, since it corrects enrichment of the mixture which otherwise would remain lean on account of air rarefaction.

Starting (Diagram C of Fig. 33)—**Knob pulled fully over:** when used for starting purposes, the device must be excluded as soon as the engine has reached a sufficient temperature to ensure smooth and regular running.

Overfeeding (Diagram C of Fig. 33)—**Knob pulled full over** as for starting: position to be resorted to **only** when the maximum power is required of the engine, i.e., **only with wide-open throttle and at high engine speeds; not to be used** when travelling with partial or variable openings of throttle.

The E.S.A. shown in Fig. 34 calls for similar operation conditions.

Progressive action starting devices

The progressive-action starting device is controlled by the panel knob and must be progressively shut off by the driver as the engine warms up. The device must be fully excluded when the engine has reached the rated operation temperature.

The starting device (**Fig. 35**) consists of valve **13** actuated by the end of rocker **19** connected through a suitable spindle to control lever **21**. By pulling the control fully over, the action of lever **21** and rocker **19** lifts valve **13** from its seat and the valve remains completely open.

Under these conditions valve **13** closes air orifice **7** and mixture orifice **9** while it uncovers both mixture orifices **10** and **12** which, through duct **6**, communicate with starting jet **25**. The valve also uncovers air orifices **16** in communication with the atmosphere via filter gauze **18** and slots **17**. Orifice **9** may communicate with the carburetor throat (with valve **13** partially open) through the central flute of the valve, through duct **8** and orifice **11** drilled in the restricted section of venturi **28**.

With the throttle in the idle position, the vacuum promoted by the starter-cranked engine causes the fuel in the starting jet housing, he starting jet **25** and reserve well **24**, to be emulsified with the air coming from orifices **22** and **23**.

Through duct **6**, orifices **10** and **12**, and duct **15** the mixture reaches the outlet, downstream of the throttle and mixes with the air entering from orifices **16**, thus permitting a prompt start.

As the device is being shut off, valve **13** progressively uncovers orifice **7** so allowing an additional amount of air to enter through valve guide **4**, giving a leaner mixture; at the same time, the valve blanks orifices **10** and **12** and air orifices **16** thus reducing the amount of incoming mixture.

In this way the less the device is inserted the leaner will the air-fuel mixture be and the quantity delivered will be reduced.

Mixture orifice **9**, duct **8** and orifice **11**, drilled in venturi **28** have the task of permitting a regular progression of acceleration even with a cold engine. By opening throttle **14** to speed up the engine, the vacuum acting on duct **15** is reduced. This would cause a reduction in the amount of fuel delivered through duct **15**, with consequent irregular running of the engine, but, through orifice **11**, duct **8** and orifice **9** (from which air is drawn when the throttle is closed) some mixture is aspirated by the vacuum formed in the restriction of the venturi consequent on the opening of the throttle, and this compensates for the reduction in delivery through duct **15**.

When the starting device is excluded, valve **13** covers also orifice **9** and prevents the entrance of mixture.

Strangler throttle (choke) type starting devices

The starting device incorporated in carburetors of the **26 DRT**

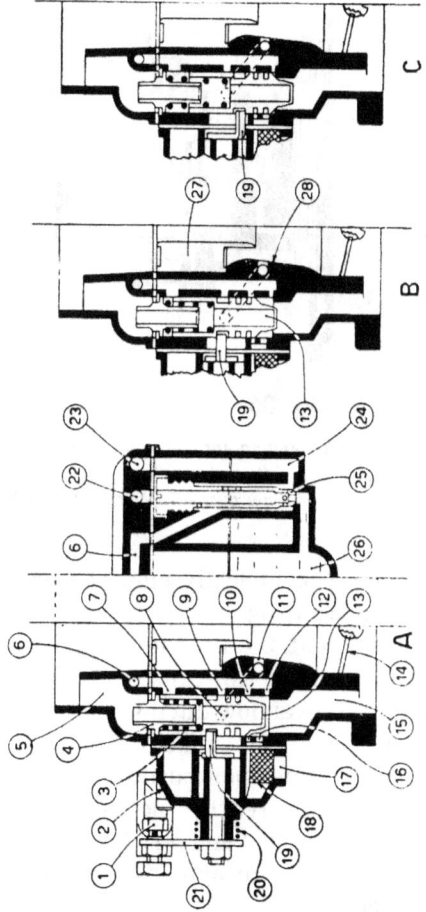

Fig. 35

1. Bowden screw - 2. Cover with bowden sheath support - 3. Spring - 4. Spring retainer and guide - 5. Air inlet - 6. Mixture duct - 7. Leaning air orifice - 8. Transition duct - 9. Transition orifice - 10. Starting mixture orifice - 11. Transition orifice - 12. Starting mixture orifice - 13. Starting valve - 14. Throttle - 15. Starting mixture duct - 16. Starting device air orifices - 17. Air intake slot - 18. Filter gauze - 19. Rocker - 20. Lever return spring - 21. Starting device control lever - 22. Starting jet emulsion air orifice - 23. Reserve well emulsion air orifice - 24. Reserve starting well - 25. Starting jet - 26. Bowl - 27. Auxiliary Venturi - 28. Primary Venturi.

type (**Fig. 36**) consist of choke **3**, housed in air horn **11**, and of primer **5** placed on the carburetor cover.

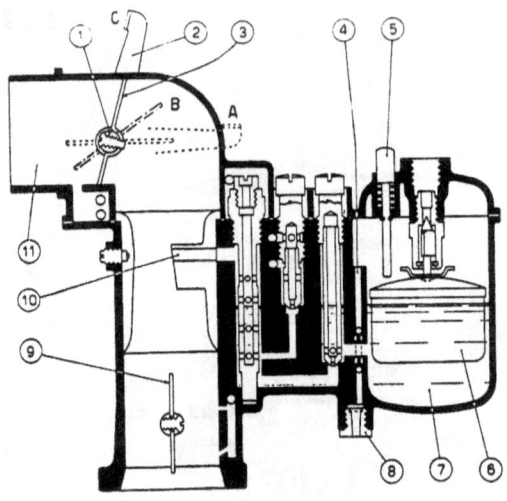

Fig. 36

1. Starting throttle shaft - **2.** Starting throttle control lever - **3.** Starting throttle (choke) **4.** Overflow duct - **5.** Primer rod - **6.** Float - **7.** Bowl - **8.** Plug for overflow duct - **9.** Main throttle - **10.** Nozzle - **11.** Air horn.

The butterfly is idle and eccentrically mounted on shaft **1** to which it is linked by a return spring.

To start the engine from cold, the float in the bowl is lowered by depressing rod **5** of the primer; this causes a rise in fuel level in bowl **7** up to the height of overflow duct **4**. Lever **2**, keyed on shaft **1** is brought to position **C** and choke **3** blanks air horn **11**. Main throttle **9** is set in the wide-open position.

The engine-promoted vacuum reaches noticeable values due to the choking caused by butterfly **3** and a rich mixture is forced out of nozzle **10** with a consequent prompt starting of the engine.

As the engine is started, due to the suction, vacuum choke **3** rotates to position **B** (against the return spring) and a regular and smooth engine operation is obtained thanks to the rich mixture it receives.

When the engine has reached a sufficient temperature to run smoothly and steadily, choke **3** is fully opened by moving lever **2** to position **A**; throttle **9** is set in the idle speed position.

The starting device of the **28TR type** carburetors (**Fig. 37**) consists of primer **3**, housed in upper body at the height of the

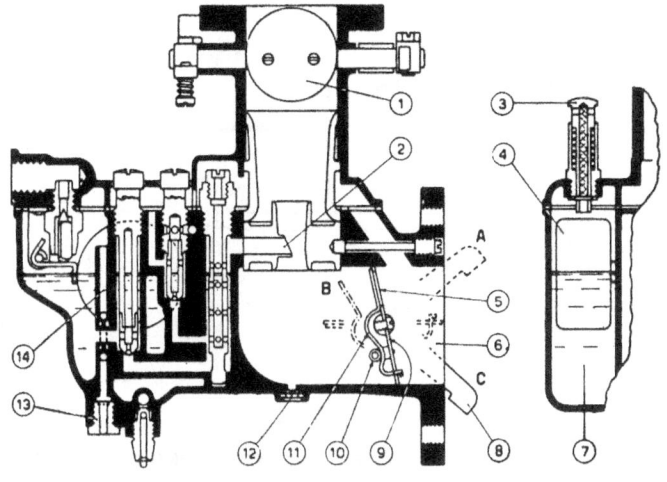

Fig. 37

float and choke **9** installed in air horn **6**. The choke is provided with a slot **5** blanked by a movable diaphragm **11** which is controlled by spring **10**.

To start the engine from cold, the fuel level in bowl **7** is caused to rise by depressing rod **3** of the primer which, in turn, pushes down float **4**. Lever **8** fixed to the shaft carrying throttle **9** is displaced in position **C** so that choke **9** blanks air horn **6**. Main throttle **1** is set in a given position by means of the controls with which the vehicle is fitted.

The engine-promoted vacuum reaches noticeable values due to the choking caused by butterfly **9** and a rich mixture is forced out of nozzle **2** with a consequent prompt starting of the engine. Once the engine is started, under the action of the vacuum diaphragm **11** takes position **B**, overcoming the action of spring **10** and opens slot **5**: this gives a sufficiently rich mixture to ensure regular and smooth engine operation. When the engine has reached the rated temperature, choke **9** is fully opened by moving lever **8** to position **A**.

ACCELERATING PUMP

An accelerating pump is usually fitted on those carburetors which, on account of their characteristics, are adjusted to give high power and, in consequence, are provided with large diameter venturis.

The accelerating pump injects into the carburetor barrel a given amount of fuel in a given time: the calibration of these two factors is the essential feature of this device.

By observing diagram **Fig. 38** it is seen that through duct **7**

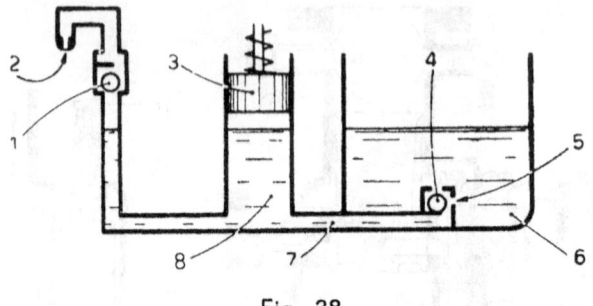

Fig. 38

1. Delivery valve - 2. Pump jet - 3. Pump plunger - 4. Inlet valve - 5. Drain hole - 6. Bowl - 7. Suction duct - 8. Pump barrel.

fuel reaches pump barrel **8** in which plunger **3** works. Inlet valve **4**, housed in bowl **6** admits fuel to the pump while delivery valve **1** checks it.

By depressing the accelerator, plunger **3** is rapidly pushed down, causing closure of the inlet valve and fuel is forced to issue through metered jet **2**. A part of the fuel, however, returns to the bowl through drain hole **5**. By releasing the accelerator pedal the vacuum caused when the plunger in the pump barrel rises, closes valve **1** so preventing the entry of air through pump jet **2**. In this way pump cylinder **8** is re-filled, fuel being drawn into the barrel through valve **4** and drain hole **5**.

Different amounts and duration of delivery are obtained by varying respectively the diameters of the pump jet and the drain hole.

In fact, by increasing the pump jet diameter a **greater** amount of fuel is injected, while by increasing the drain hole diameter **a shorter** injection will be obtained as the amount of fuel that will discharge through this hole instead of issuing through the jet will be greater.

It should be noted that variation in the metered elements of an accelerating pump brings about a variation in the pressure exerted by the plunger, and, theoretically, this would involve a number of elements which, to avoid complicating the discussion, are not mentioned here.

To determine the metering of both the pump jet and drain jet the first step is to establish the diameter of the pump jet according to the amount of fuel to be injected, then establish the diameter of the drain jet for the injection time desired.

A defective accelerating pump may bring about the following troubles:

A. **clogged pump jet**: poor pick up; crackling due to lean mixture, etc.

B. **stuck or clogged delivery valve**: incomplete filling of the pump barrel due to air infiltrations; poor pick up, crackling and impossibility of obtaining quick and successive accelerations.

C. **clogged or stuck inlet valve**: on carburetors with a large drain orifice the trouble is little felt since the pump barrel may be filled rapidly via the drain orifice. Were the drain orifice small, acceleration would be possible only at intervals because the pump would take more time to fill through the drain orifice.

D. **clogged drain jet**: fast pick up due to the greater amount of fuel injected by the pump over a longer period.

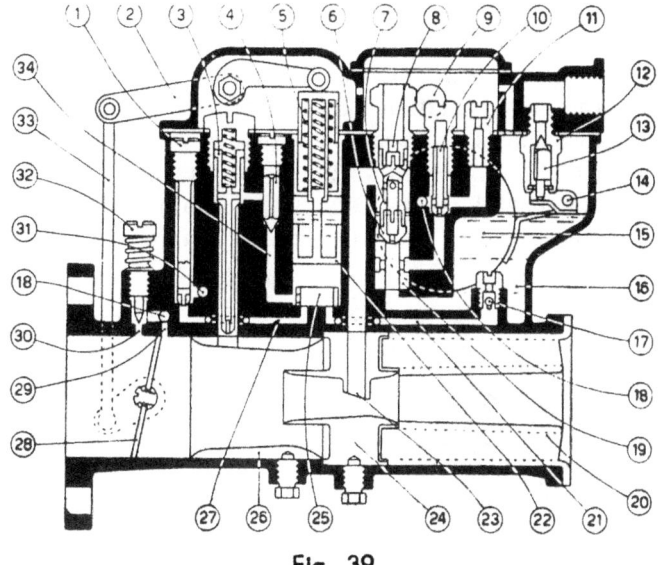

Fig. 39

1. Pump drain jet - 2. Pump control outer lever - 3. Pump jet - 4. Needle delivery valve - 5. Plunger return spring - 6. Main jet - 7. Emulsion tube - 8. Air corrector jet - 9. Dynamic air intake connection - 10. Idle speed jet - 11. Idle air jet - 12. Needle valve - 13. Valve needle - 14. Float fulcrum screw - 15. Float - 16. Bowl - 17. Pump inlet valve - 18. Idle mixture duct - 19. Idle duct and jet communication bushes - 20. Auxiliary Venturi extension - 21. Pump suction duct - 22. Pump plunger - 23. Nozzle - 24. Auxiliary Venturi - 25. Plunger stroke reduction spacer - 26. Primary Venturi - 27. Pump drain duct - 28. Throttle - 29. Transition orifice - 30. Orifice, idle jet to duct - 31. Pump drain duct - 32. Idle mixture adjustment screw - 33. Pump control rod - 34. Pump delivery duct.

Fig. 39 shows the section of a dual barrel horizontal carburetor where the accelerating pump consists of a metal plunger **22** controlled by the throttle shaft via a linkage and spring system. When the throttles close, the system frees a suitable sliding stem which, under the action of spring **5**, lifts plunger **22**: fuel is thus sucked into the pump barrel from bowl **16** through valve **17** and duct **21**. As the throttles are opened, the linkage system lowers the sliding stem against the action of spring **5** and depresses plunger **22** whose movement is governed by the pump spring housed in the stem itself.

Through dust **34** and via needle delivery valve **4**, fuel is sent to metered pump jets **3** whence it is injected into the main carburetor barrels. **Figs. 40, 41 and 42** show other details.

Fig. 40 is an inner view of a dual-barrel body where items **2** and **3** are the inlet valve and the drain jet. In **Fig. 41** item **2** is the ball inlet valve which, through a metered side hole performs also as drain jet. This simplifies the design of **Fig. 40** since a single part performs two functions.

When conditions allow, such as in the case of a large diameter drain jet, the above solution may still be simplified. In fact, in **Fig. 42** item **2** consists of a simple threaded plug on one side of which is drilled the metered drain orifice. During pump suction, filling of the barrel is ensured by the drain orifice through which, during injection, the excess fuel is also permitted to flow back to the bowl.

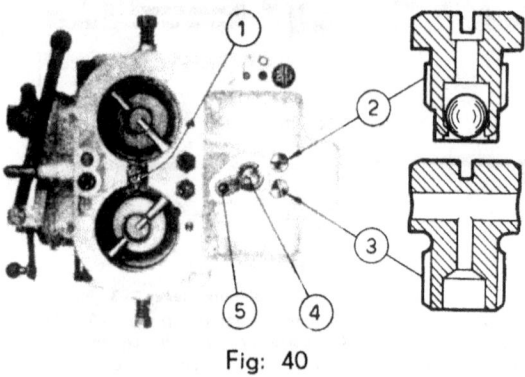

Fig: 40

1. Pump jet - 2. Inlet valve - 3. Drain jet - 4. Pump plunger - 5. **Pump control rod.**

Another solution adopted in the single throat, downdraft carburetors of the **DRNP** series is shown in **Fig. 43**. In these carburetors the acceleration pump consists of a metal plunger **5** actuated by pump control rod **4** via lever **10** with roller which is fixed to the throttle shaft.

When closing the throttle, lever **10** lifts plunger **5** by means of rod **4**. Fuel is then sucked from the bowl into the pump barrel through inlet valve **8** and duct **9**. When the throttle is opened, rod **4** is released and plunger is pushed down by spring **7**.

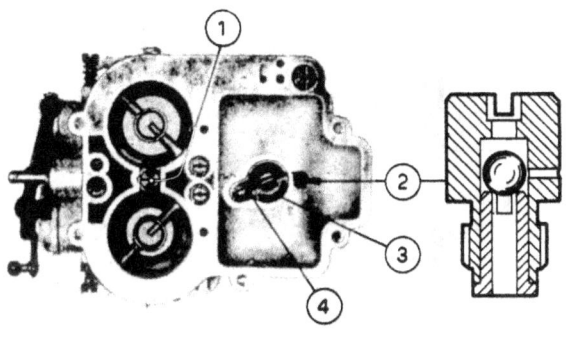

Fig. 41

1. Pump jet - 2. Inlet valve with drain hole - 3. Pump spring retaining plate 4. Pump control rod.

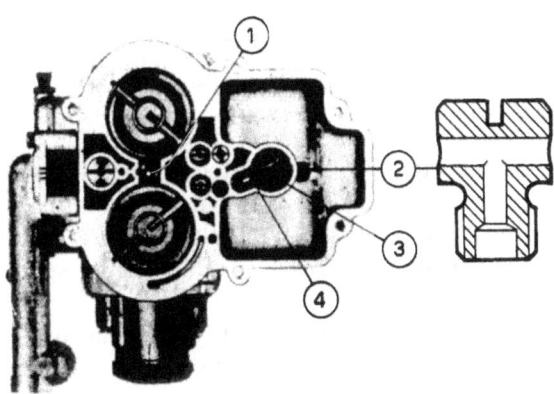

Fig. 42

1. Pump jet - 2. Pump inlet-drain jet - 3. Pump spring retaining plate - 4. Pump rod.

Through ducts **9** and **11** and valve **1** the fuel reaches metered jet **2** which sprays it into carburetor barrel. If it is desired to reduce the amount of fuel delivered by the accelerating pump, the carburetor in question may be equipped with a larger calibrated drain jet **3**.

Dual-barrel, horizontal carburetors (**Fig. 44**) are fitted with drain jet **22** housed in the pump barrel itself. In some designs drain jet **6** is derived from the delivery duct, as shown in **Fig. 45** illustrating a single-barrel, horizontal carburetor.

DUAL-BARREL CARBURETORS

In the first section of this discussion it was explained how the transition orifice, the well and the main jet enter into play

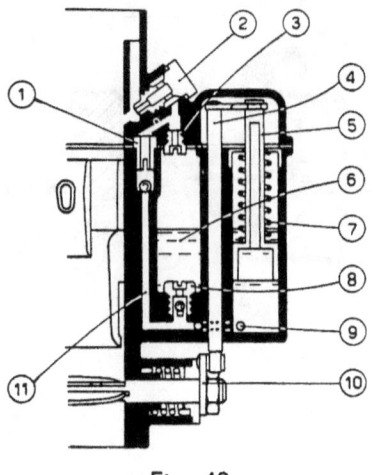

Fig. 43

1. Pump delivery valve - **2.** Pump jet - **3.** Pump drain jet - **4.** Pump control rod - **5.** Pump plunger - **6.** Fuel bowl - **7.** Pump spring - **8.** Pump inlet valve - **9.** Pump inlet-and-delivery duct - **10.** Pump control lever - **11.** Pump delivery duct.

progressively as the engine is accelerated from idle speed.

To simplify the explanation let us begin with the dual-barrel carburetor whose two throttles open simultaneously. Carburetor **DCF** illustrated in **Fig. 46** is of this type and is fit for sports cars with large piston displacement engines.

On account of its special characteristics this carburetor has no starting device. The contemporaneous opening of the two throttles is obtained by two toother sectors, on of which is adjustable.

Two ducts branch from bowl **15** and reach main jets **18**, one for each barrel.

Wells are never in communication with each other, since they may be considered as separate devices with autonomous functions.

Since the throttles open at the same time, both nozzles start supplying fuel simultaneously. Idle speed adjustment is obtained by the two screws **37**, while there are two transition orifices **38** for each barrel.

On account of the contemporaneous action, the parts intended for the two barrels must evidently have the same calibration, as against other dual-barrel carburetors where the differential opening of the throttles permits adoption of different calibration values for the primary and secondary throats.

The accelerating pump has nothing peculiar excepting pump

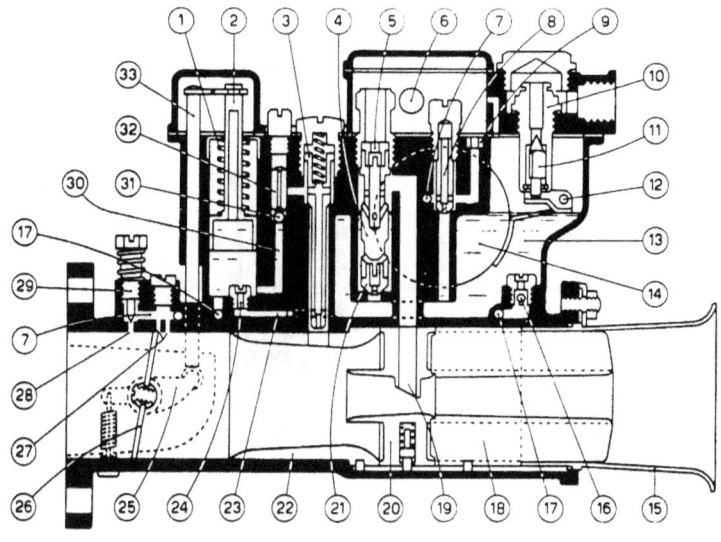

Fig. 44

1. Pump spring - **2.** Pump plunger - **3.** Pump jet - **4.** Emulsion tube - **5.** Air corrector jet - **6.** Dynamic air intake connection - **7.** Idle mixture duct - **8.** Idle jet - **9.** Idle air bush - **10.** Needle valve - **11.** Valve needle - **12.** Float fulcrum screw - **13.** Bowl - **14.** Float - **15.** Additional air horn - **16.** Pump inlet valve - **17.** Pump suction duct - **18.** Auxiliary Venturi extension - **19.** Nozzle - **20.** Auxiliary Venturi - **21.** Main jet - **22.** Primary Venturi - **23.** Pump drain duct - **24.** Pump drain jet - **25.** Pump control lever - **26.** Throttle - **27.** Transition orifices - **28.** Idle orifice to duct - **29.** Idle mixture adjustment screw - **30.** Pump delivery duct - **31.** Ball delivery valve - **32.** Ball hold-down - **33.** Pump rod.

jets **30** which have two delivery orifices; as no drain jet is provided in this carburetor, to reduce the amount of fuel delivered by the pump plunger **19** must have a hole.

The **DCF**, synchronized opening type carburetors are usually fitted on the manifolds whose duct may feed one single cylinder or a group of cylinders independently of the others. The importance of accurate location of the transition orifices in the two barrels is, therefore, apparent to prevent any unbalanced feed of the single cylinders or groups thereof.

Let us now see the diagram **(Fig. 47)** of a **DCLD** type dual-barrel carburetor with differential opening of the two throttles.

The mechanism for differential opening of the two throttles consists of toother sector **48**, idle on primary throttle shaft **30** having slot **47** into which slides lug **43** of stop sector **44** fixed to

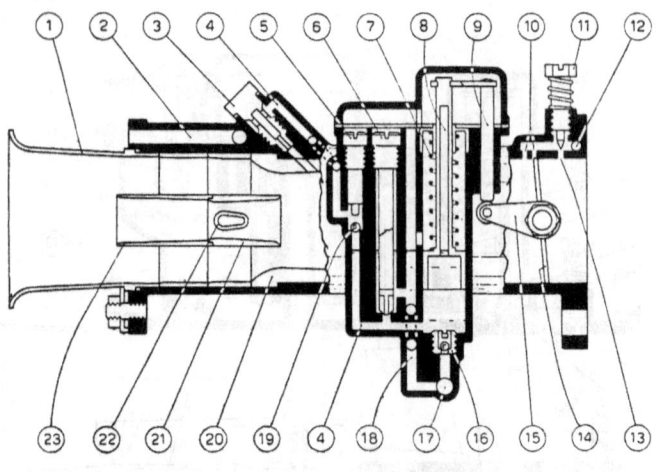

Fig. 45
1. Additional air horn - **2**. Air inlet for bowl and emulsion tube - **3**: Pump jet - **4**. Pump delivery duct - **5**. Pump ball delivery valve retaining screw - **6**. Pump drain jet - **7**. Pump spring - **8**. Pump plunger - **9**. Pump control rod - **10**. Transition orifices - **11**. Idle mixture adjustment screw - **12**. Idle mixture duct - **13**. Orifice, idle jet to duct - **14**. Throttle - **15**. Pump control lever - **16**. Pump inlet valve - **17**. Bowl communication duct - **18**. Pump drain duct - **19**. Pump delivery valve - **20**. Primary Venturi - **21**. Auxiliary Venturi - **22**. Main nozzle - **23**. Auxiliary Venturi extension.

shaft **30**. Secondary throttle shaft **33** carries toother sector **49**. By actuating throttle control lever **29**, lug **43** first slides into slot **47** of sector **48**; throttle **26**, on shaft **30**, rotates through a corresponding angle while secondary throttle **32** remains closed. Subsequently, lug **43** drives sector **48** which, through sector **49**, causes shaft **33** to rotate until both throttles are fully open.

The mechanism indicating the opening of the secondary throat consists of pushrod **42** with spring **41** housed in the toothed sector casing cover, and cam **46** having a suitable outline and fixed on primary shaft **30**. By actuating the lever controlling secondary throttle **29** when this is opened, the accelerator pedal movement is somewhat stiffened. This stiffening, due to the action of cam **46** contacting pushrod **42** warns the driver that the secondary throttle has started opening.

After overcoming this point, and up to the opening of both throttles, the operation of the accelerator pedal becomes smooth again.

The two-stage accelerating pump is incorporated to provide a smooth acceleration as each of the two throttles opens.

This pump consists of a metal plunger **23** actuated by rod **13**

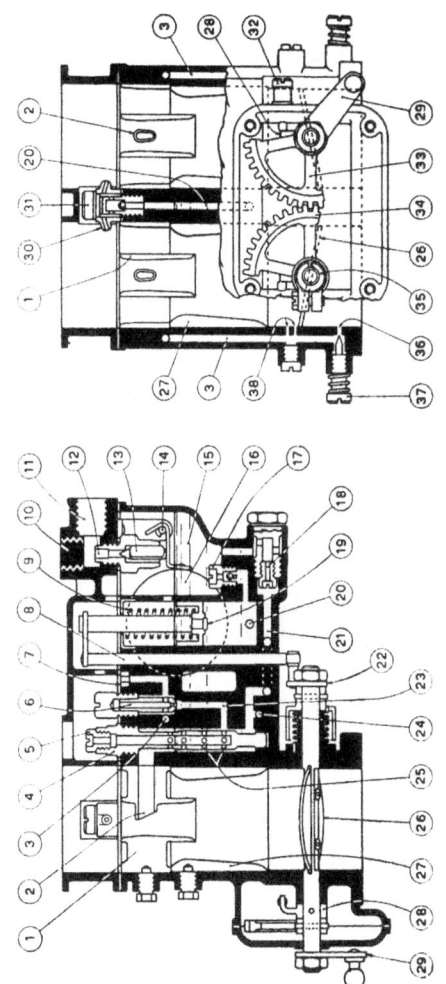

Fig. 46

1. Auxiliary Venturi - 2. Nozzles - 3. Idle mixture ducts - 4. Emulsion tubes - 5. Air correcior jets - 6. Idle mixture jets - 7. Idle air bushes - 8. Pump rod - 9. Pump spring - 10. Boss for fuel inlet connection (vertical) - 11. Fuel inlet connection (horizontal) - 12. Needle valve - 13. Valve needle - 14. Float fulcrum pin - 15. Bowl - 16. Float - 17. Pump inlet valve - 18. Main jets - 19. Pump plunger - 20. Pump delivery duct - 21. Main jets-to-wells ducts - 22. Pump control lever - 23. Idle jets-to-wells ducts - 24. Full power jets-to-wells ducts - 25. Emulsion orifices - 26. Throttles - 27. Primary Venturis - 28. Stop sectors - 29. Throttle control main lever - 30. Pump jets body - 31. Ball delivery valve - 32. Idle speed adjustment screw - 33. Stationary toothed sector - 34. Adjustable toothed sector - 35. Adjustment bush - 36. Idle jet-to-duct orifices - 37. Idle mixture adjustment screws - 38. Transition orifices.

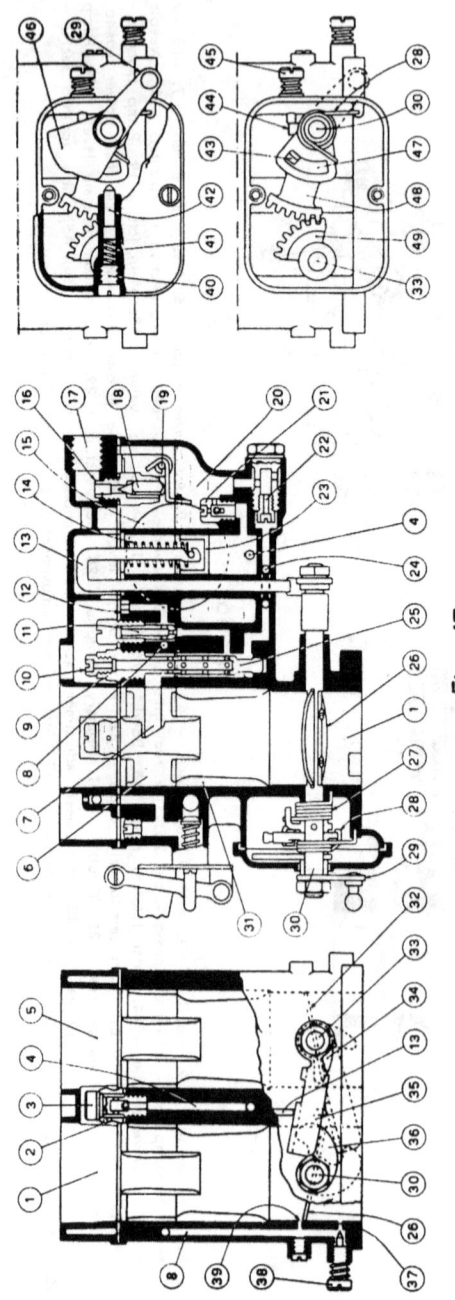

Fig. 47

1. Primary throat - 2. Pump jet - 3. Pump delivery valve - 4. Pump delivery duct - 5. Secondary throat - 6. Auxiliary Venturis - 7. Nozzles 8. Idle mixture duct - 9. Emulsion tubes - 10. Air corrector jets - 11. Idle speed jet - 12. Idle air bush - 13. Pump rod - 14. Pump spring - 15. Float - 16. Needle valve - 17. Fuel inlet connection - 18. Valve needle - 19. Float fulcrum pin - 20. Bowl - 21. Pump inlet valve with drain orifice - 22. Main jets - 23. Pump plunger - 24. Jets-to-wells ducts - 25. Emulsion orifices - 26. Primary throttle 27. Primary throttle return spring - 28. Secondary throttle return spring - 29. Throttles control main lever - 30. Primary shaft - 31. Primary throttles - 32. Secondary throttle - 33. Secondary shaft - 34. Pump control secondary lever - 35. Pump control neutral lever 36. Pump control primary lever - 37. Idle jet-to-duct orifice - 38. Idle mixture adjustment screw - 39. Transition orifice - 40. Pushrod screw - 41. Pushrod spring - 42. Pushrod indicating the opening of secondary throat - 43. Lug - 44. Stop sector - 45. Idle speed adjustment screw - 46. Cam indicating the opening of secondary throat - 47. Slot in primary sector - 48. Primary toothed sector - 49. Secondary toothed sector.

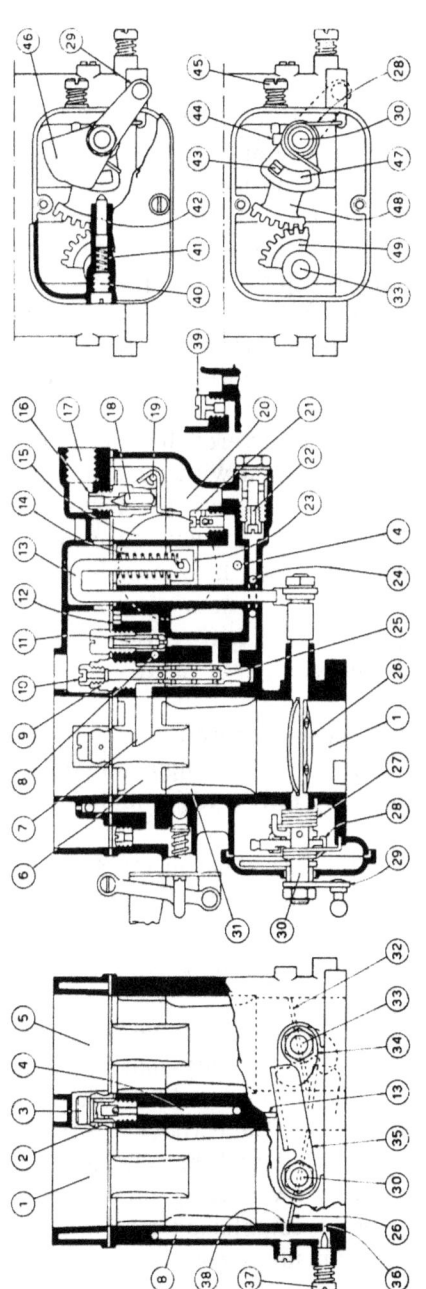

Fig. 48

1. Primary throat - 2. Pump jet - 3. Pump delivery valve - 4. Pump delivery duct - 5. Secondary throat - 6. Auxiliary Venturis - 7. Nozzles 8. Idle mixture duct - 9. Emulsion tubes - 10. Air corrector jets - 11. Idle speed jet - 12. Idle air bush - 13. Pump rod - 14. Pump spring - 15. Float - 16. Needle valve - 17. Fuel inlet connection - 18. Valve needle - 19. Float fulcrum pin - 20. Bowl - 21. Pump inlet valve with drain orifice - 22. Main jets - 23. Pump plunger - 24. Jets-to-wells ducts - 25. Emulsion orifices - 26. Primary throttle - 27. Primary throttle return spring - 28. Secondary throttle return spring - 29. Throttles control main lever - 30. Primary shaft - 31. Primary Venturis - 32. Secondary throttle - 33. Secondary shaft - 34. Pump control lever - 35. Pump control neutral lever - 36. Idle orifice to duct - 37. Idle mixture adjustment screw - 38. Transition orifice - 39. Pump inletoutlet screw - 40. Pushrod screw - 41. Pushrod spring - 42. Pushrod indicating the opening of secondary throat - 43. Lug - 44. Stop sector - 45. Idle speed adjustment screw - 46. Cam indicating the opening of secondary throat - 47. Slot in primary sector - 48. Primary toothed sector - 49. Secondary toothed sector.

45

through lever 35 neutral on secondary throttle shaft 33, lever 34 keyed to secondary throttle shaft and lever 36 fixed to primary shaft 30. As the throttles close, lever 36 lifts plunger 23 by means of lever 35 and rod 13, so that fuel is sucked from bowl 20 into the pump barrel through ball valve 21.

When the throttles are opened, shaft 30 rotates first with lever 36; lever 35 lowers until it contacts lever 34 of shaft 33 which has remained in the closed position. Under the action of spring 14, rod 13 and plunger 23 travel a given stroke and a metered amount of fuel is injected into primary barrel 1 through duct 4, valve 3 and pump metered jet 2. Subsequently, also shaft 33 rotates with lever 34; lever 35 lowers until it contacts lever 36 which is depressed: the plunger travels further and, therefore, the pump delivers a given amount of fuel also during the opening of the secondary throttle.

To reduce the amount of fuel delivered by the accelerating pump, inlet valve 21 may be furnished with a lateral calibrated hole which discharges the excess fuel into the bowl.

Contrary to the dual-barrel, simultaneous throttle opening carburetors, the carburteors described here may have a different metering of the elements for the primary and the secondary throat. This should be kept in mind when servicing or cleaning carburetors in order not to interchange or modify the calibrated parts.

It must again be said that these carburetors may be installed exclusively on intake manifolds with a single intake chamber so that idle speed is adjusted by only one jet and one mixture adjustment screw.

Next in the series are the dual-barrel carburetors that, though having barrels of the same diameter and differently calibrated parts for the two throats, have an accelerating pump which injects fuel in the primary throat when the secondary throttle is opened.

The pump (Fig. 48) consists of a metal plunger 23 actuated by rod 13 through lever 35 (neutral on primary shaft 30) and lever 34 keyed to secondary shaft 33. As the throttles close, lever 34 lifts plunger 23 by means of lever 35 and rod 13 so that fuel is sucked from bowl 20 into the pump barrel through valve 21.

By acting on throttles control lever 29, primary throttle 26 opens up to the stiffening point established by the secondary throat opening indicator mechanism; secondary throttle 32 remains closed. During this first stage of acceleration **the pump remains inactive.** Subsequently, as secondary throttle 32 is opened, secondary shaft 33 rotates with lever 34 and causes neutral lever **35** to lower; under the action of spring **14** both rod **13** and plunger **23** travel a given stroke and fuel is injected into primary barrel **1** through duct **4**, valve **3** and pump metered jet **2**.

Should it be necessary to adopt a noticeably large diameter drain orifice, valve **21** may be replaced by screw **39** whose orifice, valve **21** may be replaced by screw **39** whose orifice performs as inlet and drain port.

Carburetors having barrels of the same diameter have been considered so far, but other carburetors exist, where the diameter of the primary throat is notably smaller than the secondary throat. An example is carburetor **DCZC** installed as standard equipment on **Citroen DS19 cars.**

Fig. **49** illustrates how this carburetor incorporates the peculiarity of having a single idle mixture adjusting screw **25** even though there are two idle speed jets. The primary throat idle orifice **32** is **fixed,** i.e., has no means of adjustment.

Other types of carburetors are those with four barrels and are used mainly for racing cars. Their throttles are controlled by parallel shafts whose rotation is synchronized by a pair of toothed sectors (**Fig. 50**).

Every throat is fitted with a metered orifice **15** for idle operation and every orifice is provided with its own adjusting screw.

No starting device is provided in the four-barrel carburetors (this principle being common to almost all racing engine carburetors).

This particular type of carburetor is provided with additional air intakes in order to increase the velocity of incoming air and with extended auxiliary venturis having the purpose of dampening the engine aspiration pulsations thus preventing the rejection of mixture at given RPM rates.

HIGH SPEED DEVICE

Figs. 39 and 51 show two types of dual-barrel, horizontal carburetors for racing cars. In these carburetors the accelerating pump delivery valve performs also as a high speed device according to this principle: when (see **Fig. 51**) the vacuum in the carburetor barrels is strong enough to lift hold-down weight **32** and ball **31** from its set, a given amount of fuel is sucked into the primary barrels through inlet valve **16**, ducts **17** and **30**, and pump jets **3**. This causes an enrichment of the mixture with consequent increased power of the engine. Only when the engine rpm are reduced will the vacuum action of the pump jet become weaker and both valve **31** and holddown weight **32** will then fall back into their seat through gravity.

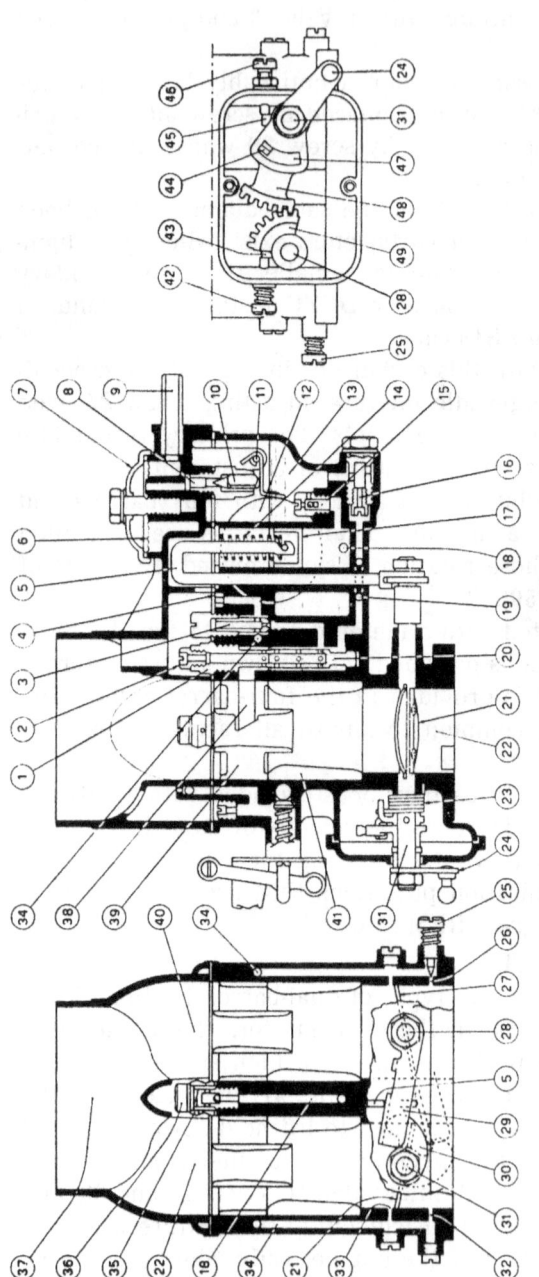

Fig. 49

1. Emulsion tubes - **2.** Air corrector jets - **3.** Idle jets - **4.** Idle air bushes - **5.** Pump control rod - **6.** Pump fulcrum pin - **7.** Filter cover - **8.** Needle valve - **9.** Fuel inlet connection - **10.** Valve needle - **11.** Pump plunger - **12.** Float - **13.** Bowl - **14.** Pump spring - **15.** Inlet valve with drain orifice - **16.** Main jets - **17.** Pump throat - **18.** Pump delivery duct - **19.** Main jets-to-wells ducts - **20.** Emulsion orifices - **21.** Primary throttle - **22.** Primary throat - **23.** Pump throat return spring - **24.** Throttles control lever - **25.** Idle mixture adjustment screw - **26.** Idle orifice to secondary throat - **27.** Secondary throttle - **28.** Secondary shaft - **29.** Pump control neutral lever - **30.** Pump control lever - **31.** Primary shaft - **32.** Idle orifice to primary throat - **33.** Transition orifices - **34.** Idle mixture duct - **35.** Pump jet - **36.** Pump delivery valve - **37.** Air horn - **38.** Nozzles - **39.** Auxiliary Venturis - **40.** Secondary throat - **41.** Primary Venturis - **42.** Secondary shaft idle speed adjusting screw - **43.** Secondary shaft stop sector - **44.** Sector lug - **45.** Primary shaft stop sector - **46.** Primary throat idle speed adjustment screw - **47.** Primary sector slot - **48.** Primary toothed sector - **49.** Secondary toothed sector.

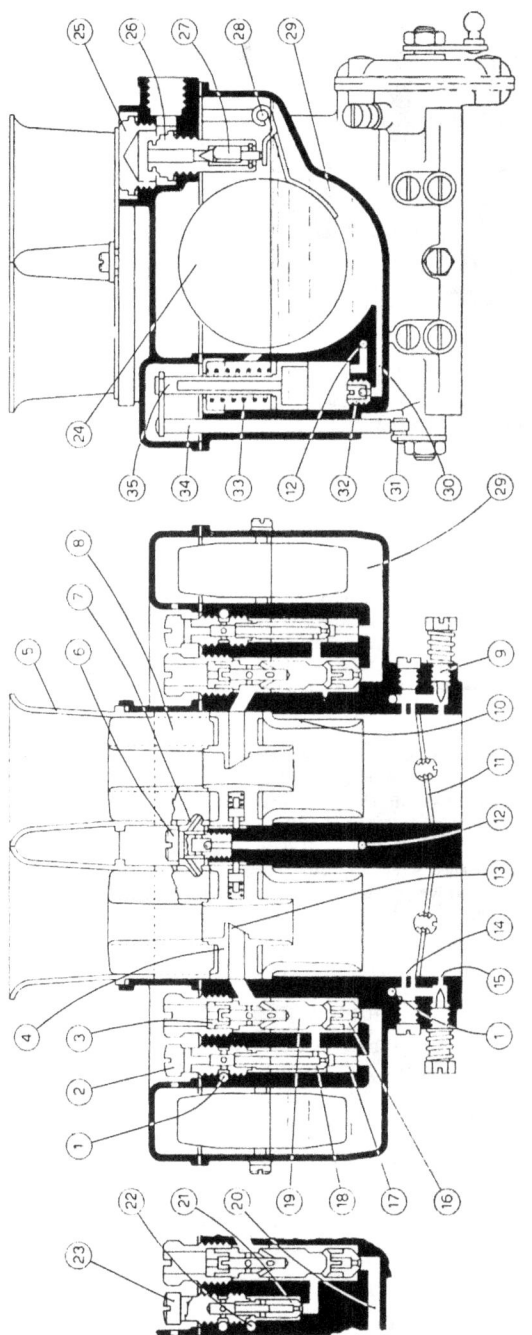

Fig. 50

1. Idle mixture ducts - 2. Idle jet holders - 3. Air corrector jets - 4. Auxiliary Venturis - 5. Additional air horns - 6. Ball delivery valve - 7. Pump jet bodies - 8. Auxiliary Venturi extensions - 9. Idle mixture adjustment screws - 10. Primary Venturis - 11. Throttles - 12. Pump delivery duct - 13. Nozzles - 14. Transition orifices - 15. Idle orifices to duct - 16. Main jets - 17. Idle mixture bushes (two-stage system) - 18. Idle jets (two-stage system) - 19. Emulsion tubes - 20. Duct to bowl - 21. Idle speed jets - 22. Idle air ducts - 23. Idle jet holders - 24. Float - 25. Needle valve inspection plug - 26. Needle valve - 27. Valve needle - 28. Float fulcrum screws - 29. Bowl - 30. Pump inlet duct - 31. Pump control lever - 32. Pump inlet valve - 33. Pump spring - 34. Pump control rod - 35. Piston plunger.

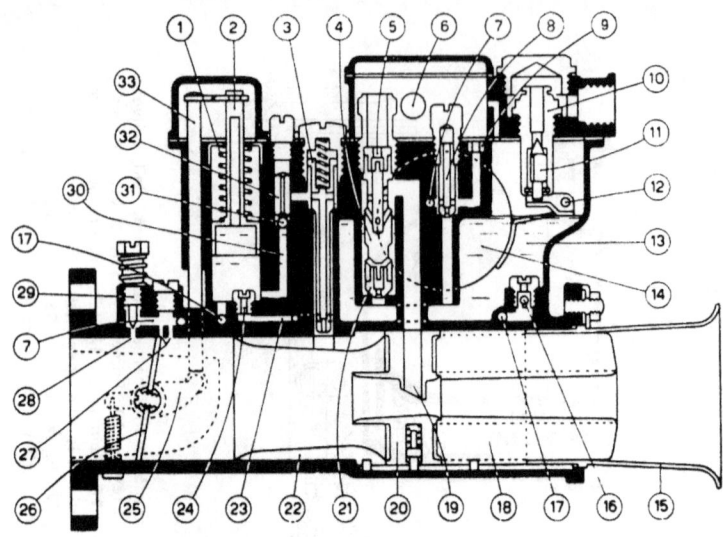

Fig. 51

1. Pump spring - **2.** Pump plunger - **3.** Pump jet - **4.** Emulsion tube - **5.** Air corrector jet - **6.** Dynamic air intake connection - **7.** Idle mixture duct - **8.** Idle jet - **9.** Idle air bush - **10.** Needle valve - **11.** Valve needle - **12.** Float fulcrum pin - **13.** Bowl - **14.** Float - **15.** Additional air horn - **16.** Pump inlet valve - **17.** Pump suction duct - **18.** Auxiliary Venturi extension - **19.** Nozzle - **20.** Auxiliary Venturi - **21.** Main jet - **22.** Primary Venturi - **23.** Pump drain duct - **24.** Pump drain jet - **25.** Pump control lever - **26.** Throttle - **27.** Transition orifices - **28.** Idle orifice to duct - **29.** Idle mixture adjustment screw - **30.** Pump delivery duct - **31.** Ball delivery valve - **32.** Ball hold-down - **33.** Pump rod.

In **Fig. 39** it is needle **4** which performs as the high speed device. Its operation is still dependent on vacuum, as for the ball valve mentioned above. The needle weight is calibrated to permit the rising of the needle only at the required RPM rates.

FULL-POWER DEVICE

This device consists (**Fig. 52**) of valve **24** and metered jets **20**.

For throttle opening position between ⅔ and total opening, plunger **15** is depressed by spring **9** opening full-power valve **24** and so allows the fuel (metered by jets **20**) to flow from the bowl through inlet valve **19** and ducts **21**, thus enriching the mixture drawn in by the engine.

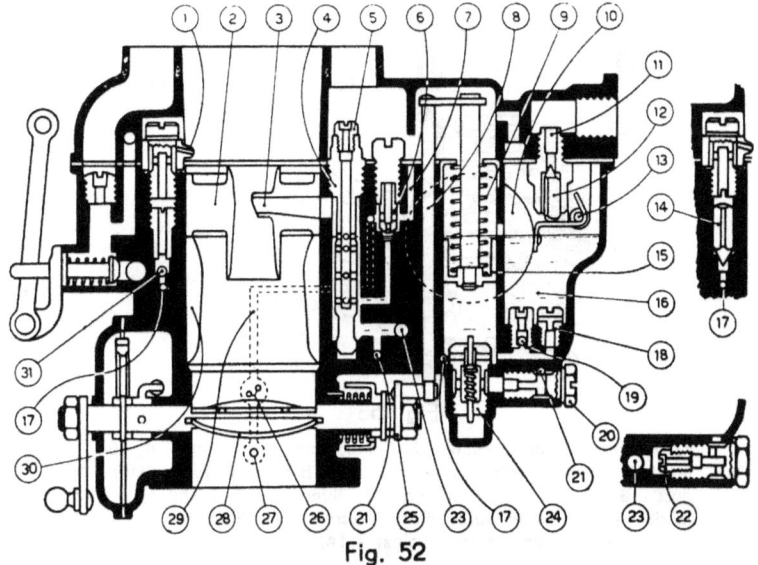

Fig. 52

1. Pump jet body - 2. Auxiliary Venturi - 3. Nozzle - 4. Emulsion tube - 5. Air corrector jet - 6. Idle speed jet - 7. Idle air orifice - 8. Pump rod - 9. Pump spring - 10. Float - 11. Needle valve - 12. Valve needle - 13. Float fulcrum pin - 14. Needle delivery valve - 15. Pump plunger - 16. Bowl - 17. Pump duct - 18. Pump drain jet - 19. Pump inlet valve - 20. Full power jet - 21. Full power duct - 22. Main jet - 23. Jet-to-well duct - 24. Full power-valve - 25. Pump control lever - 26. Transition orifices - 27. Idle orifice to duct - 28. Throttle 29. Idle mixture duct - 30. Primary Venturi - 31. Ball delivery valve.

A comparison between the high-speed and the full-power devices discloses that the former intervents only when the vacuum is such as to cause the rising of the pump delivery valve needle while the latter is operative even when the vehicle moves at average or low speeds but with both throttles wide open.

ANTI-DIESLING DEVICE

Its purpose is that of shutting off the fuel supply to the engine as soon as the ignition is switched off, to prevent the engine from continuing to run by self-ignition due to overheating resulting from prolonged operation under heavy load.

This device **(Fig. 53)** consists of solenoid **4**, spring **12** and knob **1** which, through a suitable rod, controls plunger **9** in which milling **8** is machined. Solenoid **4** is fed by the low-voltage circuit through the ignition switch on the instrument panel by means of laminae **3** and **14**, and finger **2** fixed to knob **1**.

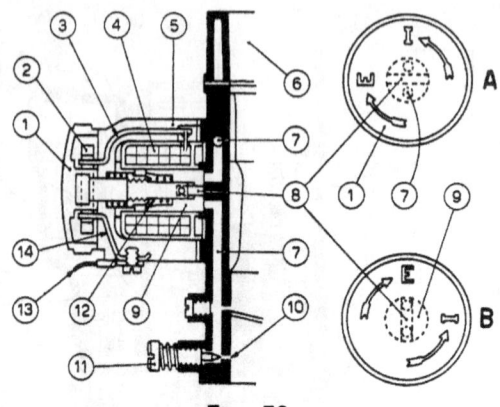

Fig. 53

1. Interceptor control knob - **2.** Contact lug - **3.** Lamina - **4.** Solenoid - **5.** Interceptor body - **6.** Primary barrel - **7.** Idle mixture duct - **8.** Communication milling - **9.** Plunger - **10.** Idling orifice to duct - **11.** Idle mixture adjusting screw - **12.** Plunger spring - **13.** Interceptor connecting terminal - **14.** Lamina.

When the device is in operation **(diagram A)** letter **I** "**inserted**" is turned uppermost and milling **8** is located between the two ports of duct **7**. As the ignition key is inserted in the switch to start the engine, the circuit closes, solenoid **4** is excited and by overcoming the load of spring **12** lifts plunger **9** thus establishing a communication between the two portions of duct **7**. The fuel may thus regularly flow to the cylinders.

When the key is withdrawn to switch off the ignition, the current to solenoid **4** is cut off; the solenoid is demagnetized, plunger **9** retracts under the action of spring **12** and the communication between the two portions of duct **7** is blanked off: the engine stops immediately even if overheated to the point that self-ignition may occur.

Should it be desired to exclude the device, knob **1** must be rotated 90°, i.e., with letter **E** ("**excluded**") uppermost **(diagram B)**. In this position finger **2** breaks the contact between laminae **3** and **14**, plunger **9** leaves a passage between the two portions of duct **7** via milling **8** and idle mixture flows regularly to the engine.

WEBER CARBURETORS TYPICAL INSTALLATIONS, SET UP, AND ADJUSTMENTS

ALFA ROMEO
GIULIA 1600 TI SUPER SEDAN AND TI SPRINT GT SEDAN
GIULIA 1600 SPIDER ROADSTER, 1600 VELOCE & GT

ALFA ROMEO

GIULIA TI SUPER SEDAN AND TI SPRINT GT SEDAN
GIULIA 1600 SPIDER ROADSTER, 1600 VELOCE & GT.

A single C 32 PAIA-7 Solex carburetor is used on the standard 1600 TI sedan. On the Super, twin dual throat Weber 45 DCOE 14 carburetors are used and on the Sprint GT and Giulia Spider Roadster a pair of dual throat Weber 40 DCOE 4 units are used. 1600 Veloce & GT use Weber 40 DCOE-2 and 40 DCOE-4 respectively. The two Weber DCOE units are essentially the same for tuning and assembly-disassembly purposes, therefore, the 45 DCOE will be covered in detail as typical to both it and the 40 DCOE.

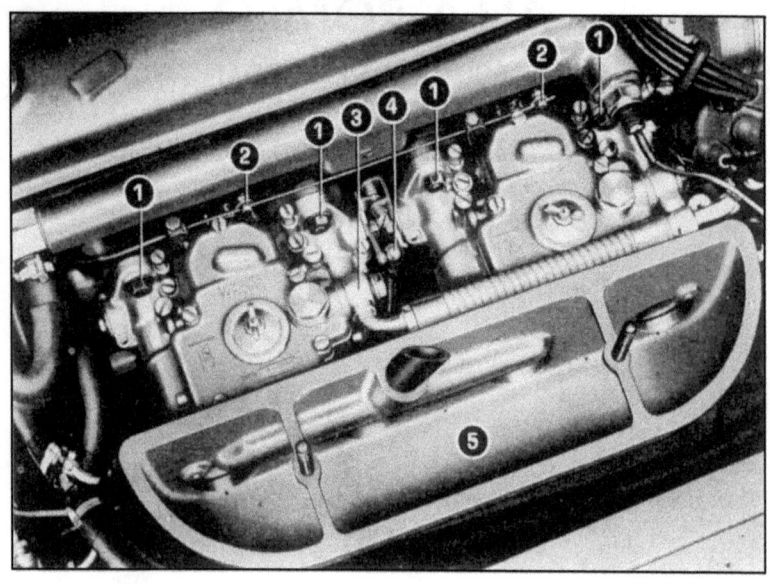

WEBER 45 DCOE 14

REMOVAL FROM THE ENGINE
Remove:
1. Air intake cover, after removing intake tube clamps.
2. Air intake box **5**.
3. Choke wire **2** from the carburetor body.

4. Throttle control **4** from the carburetor.
5. Fuel feed pipe **3**.
6. Nuts **1** from the studs which fix the carburetor body to the manifold.

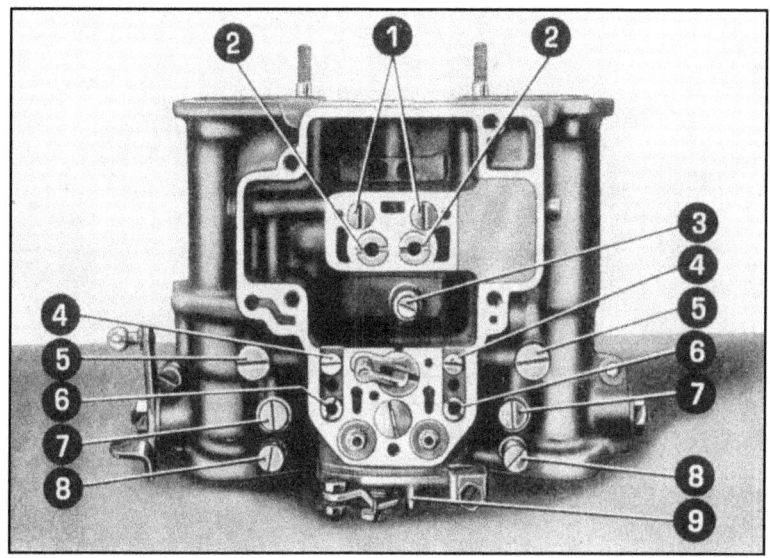

DISMANTLING

Remove the cover from the carburetor and disassemble the fuel filter screen, the float, needle valve and gasket.

Warning: Lift off the cover very carefully so as not to distort the float.

Then, remove:
1. Idling jet holder and jet.
2. Main jet.
3. Inlet valve from the acceleration pump (screw plugs, ball seats and balls).
4. Acceleration pump delivery valve.
5. Acceleration pump jet.
6. Choke jet.
7. Inspection screws from the steady acceleration port trap.
8. Idling mixture adjustment screw.
9. Choke assembly.
10. Acceleration pump, after detaching:
11. Spring plate (use a screwdriver).
12. Choke valves with springs and spring seats (after detaching circlips).

Unless absolutely necessary, it is inadvisable to remove the throttle valve spindle. If this operation has to be performed:
A. remove the small cover as shown;
B. disengage the spindle return spring after removing the retaining plate **1**;
C. mark the positions of the throttle valves with respect to the spindle and of the spindle to the body of the carburetor;
D. detach the throttle valves from the spindle;

E. remove the locking pin **2** from the pump control lever;
F. unscrew the nut **3** and withdraw from the spindle the control lever with its shim, the spring retaining cover, the spring and the dust cover;
G. withdraw the spindle from the opposite side, at the same time removing the acceleration pump control lever, the spring and the retaining cover.

13. Remove the end cover from the float chamber, situated in the lower part of the carburetor.

14. Remove the mixers and the venturis after having loosened the setscrews.

CLEANING

Very carefully wash with petrol and clean with compressed air all the parts dismantled, being careful to remove all impurities which may have been deposited in the filter trap bottom, the float chamber bottom, in the passages or in the calibrated jet bores, the air restrictors (air calibrators), the mixture tubes, the idling mixture passages, steady acceleration ports, etc.

Warning: when cleaning jets and calibrated bores in general, **never use metal needles or other tools** which may change the diameters of the bores.

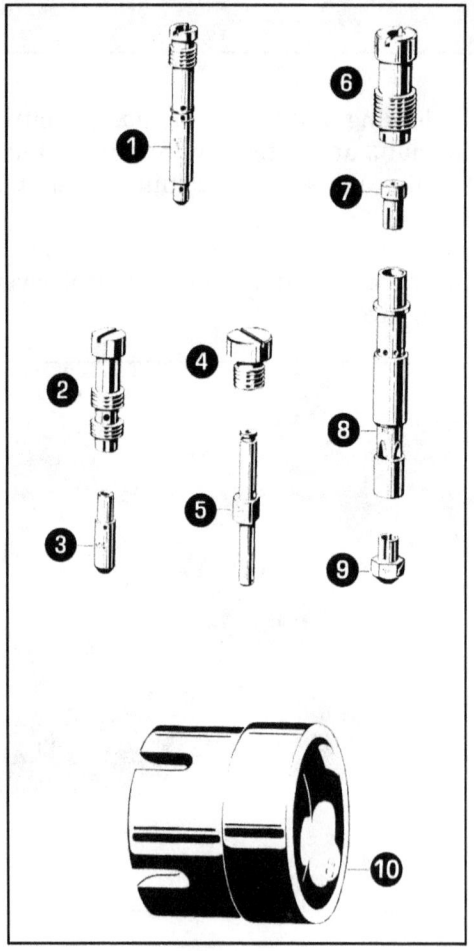

INSPECTION AND CHECKING

Check that the numbers stamped on the jets are in agreement with those given in the table.

Choke
1 jet 65

Idling
2 jet holder .... —
3 jet 55
    axial hole 220
    air calibrator hole 120

Acceleration
4 screw plug .... —
5 pump jet 50

Running
6 main jet holder .... —
7 air calibrator 180
8 mixture tube (8 radial holes) 100
9 main jet   summer 115
           winter 120
10 venturi .... 30.00 mm

NOTE:

The diffusing jets, air calibrator pets, or restrictors), etc. are marked in the position showns in the figures.

The float level should be set by following the instructions below:

1. Make sure that the float is of the correct weight (26 gm - .9 oz.), that is is not leaking anywhere and is not dented, and that it can rotate freely about the pivot pin.

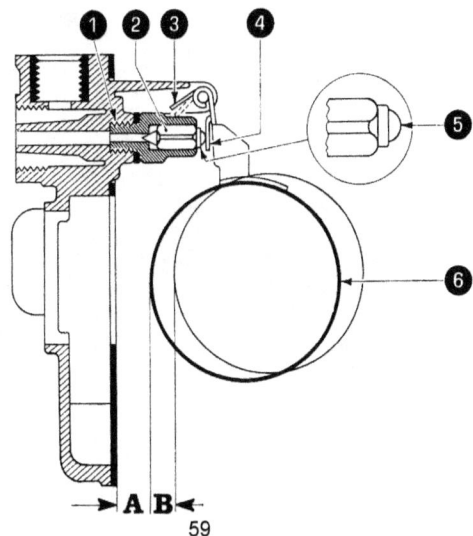

The weight of the float cannot be altered; consequently, haphazard repairs (tinning, etc.) can impair the proper operation of the float itself.

2. Check that the needle valve **1** is well screwed into the seating and that the spring loaded ball **5**, part of the needle **2**, is not jammed.

3. Hold the carburetor cover in a vertical position as shown in the figure so that the float **6** does not depress the ball **5** mounted on the needle **2**.

With the cover vertical and the float tongue **4** in light contact with the needle ball, the two floats should be at a distance from the cover joining surface of $A = 8.5$ mm (.33 in.) with the gasket fitted and well stuck to the cover.

4. When the level has been set, check that the travel **B** of the float is 6.5 mm (.26 in.) adjusting if necessary the position of the float pivot tail **3**.

5. If the float position is not correct, alter the position of the float tongue itself to achieve the correct level, making sure that the tongue remains at right angle to the needle centerline and that its contact surface has no notches which might impede the free movement of the needle.

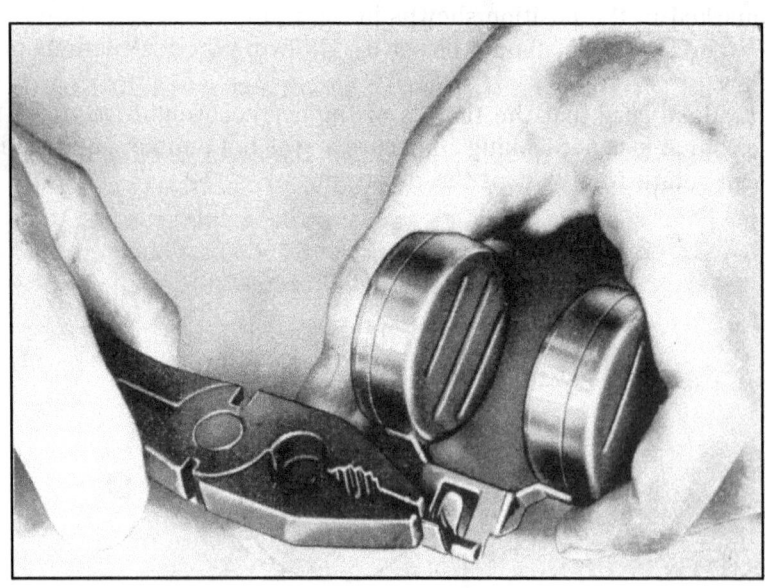

6. Then fit the carburetor cover and check that the float can move freely without friction on the walls of the float chamber.

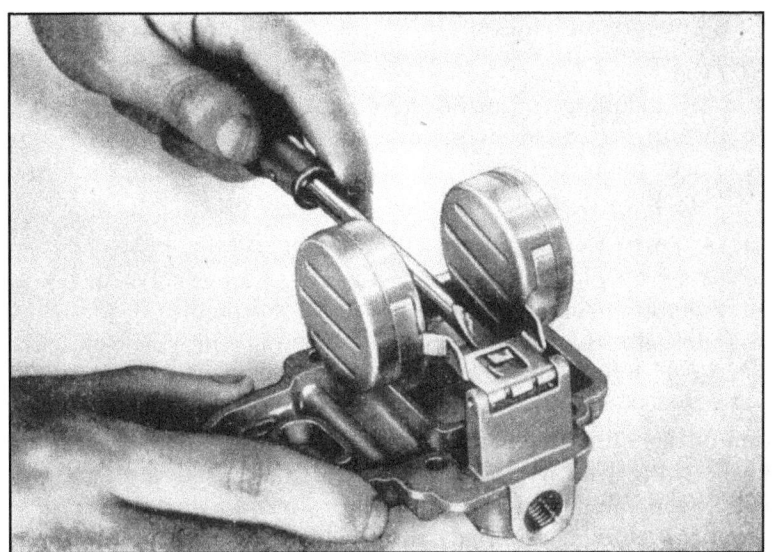

PRECAUTIONS

The float level should be checked whenever the float or the needle valve has ben changed. In the latter case it is also advisable to change the gasket.

The adjustment described above will correspond to a fuel level, from the upper face of the float chamber, of 29 ± .5 mm (1.14 ± .02 in.).

This level can be checked as shown under "Adjustment of Control Linkage."

Check that the joining surfaces or the cover itself and on the carburetor body are in good condition. If necessary, where it is possible to grind without impairing the values which are the basis of the calibration of the carburetor, (gasoline level with respect to the positions of the jets), remove the minimum nec-

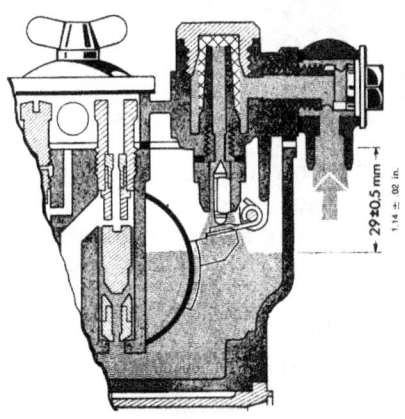

essary amount of material.

NOTE:

When grinding is finished the whole of the carburetor must be carefully cleaned to remove all traces of dust which may have been deposited in the channels, traps, etc. during the work.

Check the condition of all seals.

REASSEMBLING THE CARBURETOR

The carburetor should be reassembled in reverse order of disassembly, bearing in mind the following points:

1. Lubricate the ball bearings supporting the throttle valve spindle with bearing grease.
2. Before the spindle is fitted to the body and to avoid distortion of the spindle while tightening the nut at the end opposite. to the control lever, it is advisable to tighten this nut in a vise fitted lead jaws, gripping the spindle itself close to the nut to avoid damaging the milled seatings for the throttle valves.
3. The reference marks made on the throttle valves and on the spindle must coincide.

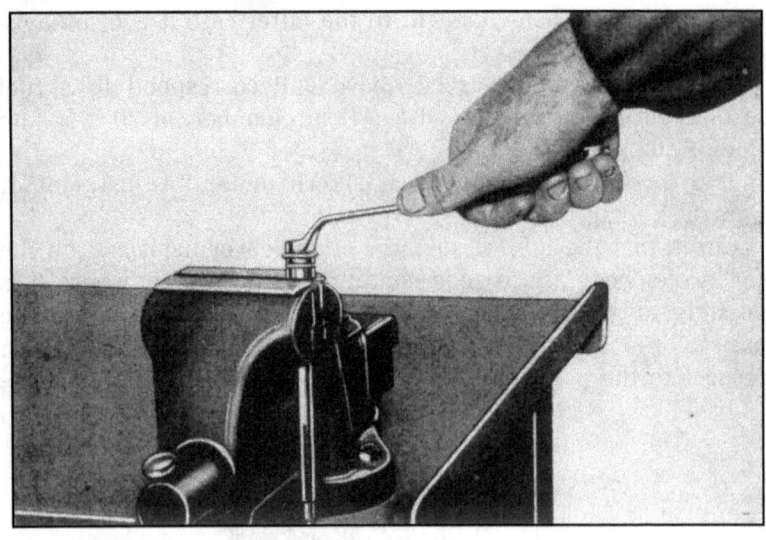

4. Before fitting the throttle valves to the spindle, fully unscrew the opening adjusting screws.
5. Fit, center and secure one throttle at a time, taking particular care with the centering so as to obtain a proper fit with the throttles in contact with the bores of the barrels. With a correctly centered throttle, if it is looked at in back light, no light should be seen around the valve. Some light may be tolerated in the areas close to the spindle.

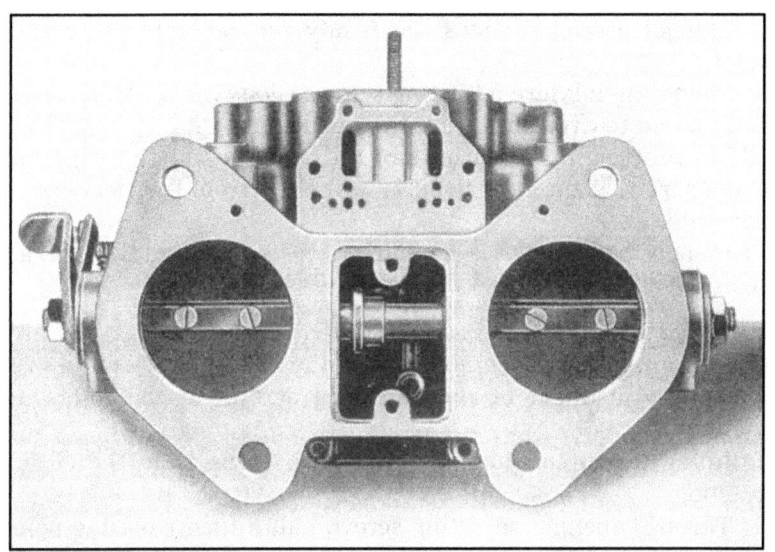

When the first valve has been fitted, the second should be fitted in the same way. Before fitting the return spring, check that the spindle complete with valves rotates freely.

6. To refit the acceleration pump on the body press on the spring plate with a screwdriver so as to insert the plate into its proper groove on the body.

7. To refit the two plungers of the choke assembly, press with a screwdriver on the retainer rings so as to force them into their respective grooves on the body.

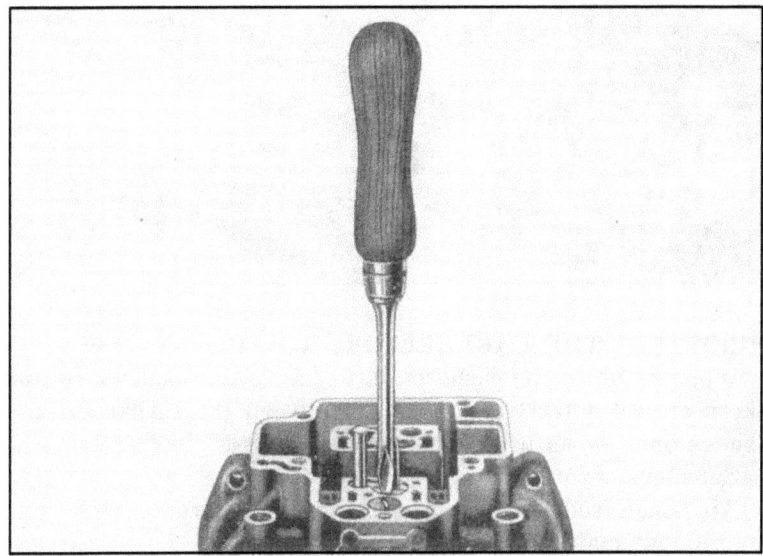

8. The jet assemblies must be firmly secured into the carburetor.

9. The idling mixture adjusting screws should never be screwed fully home to avoid breaking the needle seat.

10. In refitting to the carburetor the cover complete with float, make sure that the float itself is well clear from the float chamber walls.

11. When reassembly is complete, check the tightness of all seals to ensure that there will be no leakage.

PROVISIONAL IDLING ADJUSTMENT

Before refitting the carburetor to the engine carry out a provisional adjustment of the adjusting screws in the following manner:

1. Idling mixture adjusting screw: two turns from the closed position.

2. Throttle opening adjusting screw: half a turn from the point of contact.

REFITTING THE CARBURETORS TO THE ENGINE

When refitting the carburetors to the engine **make sure that there are no defects in the joints between the carburetor and the engine,** so as to prevent seepage of air downstream the carburetors.

Any such seepage would cause irregular carburetion and consequent malfunctioning of the engine.

Alignment of throttles, idling adjustment and adjustment of control linkage

To obtain good matching of the two carburetors and correct adjustment of the control linkage, proceed as follows:

A. **Alignment of throttles:**
1. Disconnect the control linkage **T** from the carburetors.
2. Almost fully loosen the screws **F** and **S** until the throttle control lever stop is just making contact against the boss.
3. Then screw in the screw **S** until contact is made, so that the throttles in the two carburetors are aligned.
4. Unscrew in screw **F** until it makes contact, then screw it in a further half turn.

B. **Idling speed adjustment**

When the throttles have been aligned and still with the control linkage disconnected:
1. Check that the spark plugs and the ignition system are in good order.
2. Unscrew the screws **M** about one turn from the closed position.
3. Start the engine and warm it up.
4. Operate the throttles a few times, making sure that they function without sticking.
5. Screw in progressively the screms **M** until the engine runs smoothly.
6. Unscrew the screw **F** very slowly until the engine is idling at 600 to 700 rpm.

If the engine starts to race, tighten the screws **M** slightly. **On no account should these screws be screwed right down.**
ADJUSTMENT OF CONTROL LINKAGE

When the throttles have been aligned and the idling adjusted, proceed with the adjustment of the carburetor control linkage.

For this purpose the adjustable rod should have been reconnected to the throttle control lever. Having slackened the locknut on the rod, adjust rod length so that there is a slight preload on the lever itself when the pedal is in the rest position.

Checking the fuel level in the float chambers with the carburetors on the car

If it is necessary to carry out this check, level the car and for each carburetor carry out the following operations:
1. Remove the jet inspection cover and both main jets.
2. By means of a syringe, draw off from the wells a quantity of gasoline sufficient to cause a substantial lowering of the level.
3. Refit the cover and run the engine at idling speed for some seconds.
4. Again remove the cover and measure with a gauge the fuel level with respect to the upper face of the float chamber.

The level should be $29 \pm .5$ mm ($1.14 \pm .02$ in.). If this is not so, adjust the float and check the tightness of the needle valve,

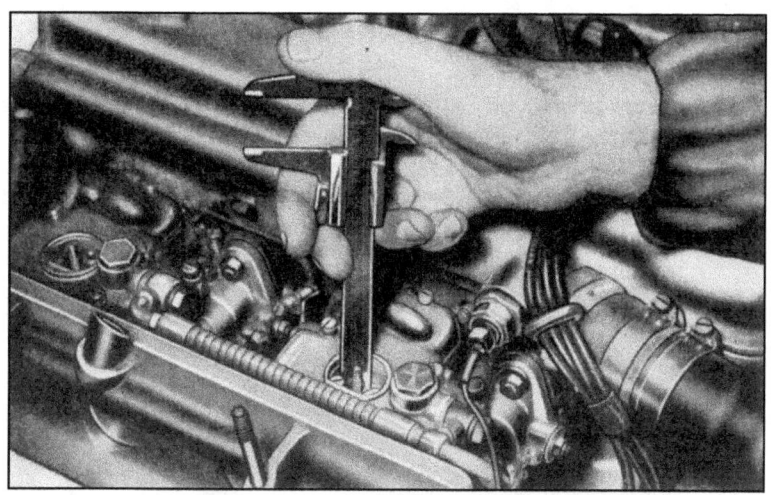

renewing it if there is any leak.

WEBER 40 DCOE 4 CARBURETOR

For overhaul and adjustment of the carburetors, see Weber 45 DCOE 14.

Adjustment data:
1 Main jets (with ⅛" dia. ball) 127
   Main air restrictor jets 220

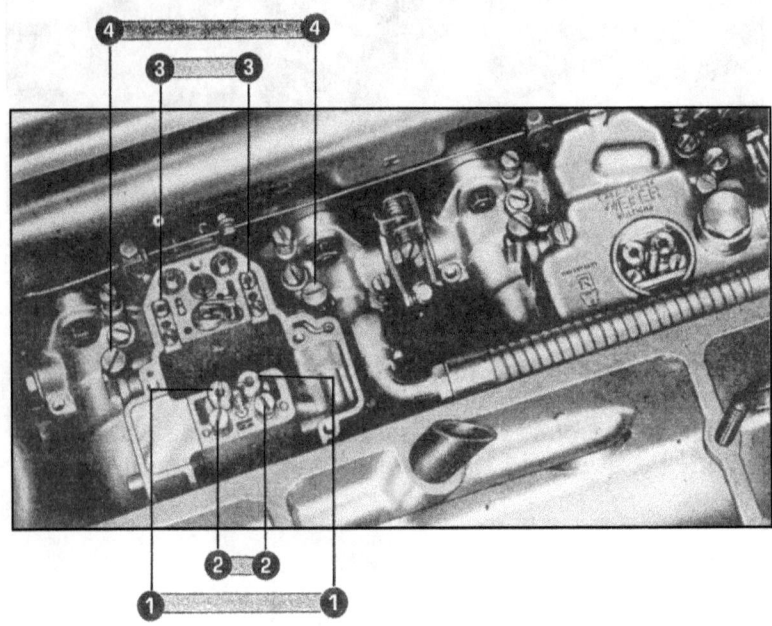

2 Idling jets 50
   axial hole 150
   air restrictor jet 120
3 Choke jets F5 65
4 Acceleration pump jets 35
   Venturis .... 30.00 mm

WEBER CARBURETORS TYPICAL INSTALLATIONS, SET UP, AND ADJUSTMENTS

FIAT

500, 600, 600D, 1100, 103D, 1100D
1200 GL, 100H, 1500 CABRIOLET

FIAT

The Fiat line is equipped with Weber carburetors. Operating principles and construction details will be found under the heading 'Weber Theory and Practice' elsewhere in this book.

Applications and critical float level dimensions of various carburetors are given below:

Model	Carburetor	Float "X"	Level* "Z"
500	26 IMB 4	7	14
600	22 IM	5	12
	26 IM	7	15
600 D	28 ICP	7	14
	28 ICI 1	7	14
	28 ICP 5	7	14
1100/103D	32 IMPE	9	16
1100 D	32 IMPE 4 & 5	9	16
1200 G.L., 100 H	36 DCD 3	5	13.5
	36 DCD 7	5	13.5
1500 Cabriolet	28/36 DCD 20	5	13.5

*DIRECTIONS FOR LEVELING THE FLOAT

It is essential that the following general directions be carried out to obtain correct levelling of the float:

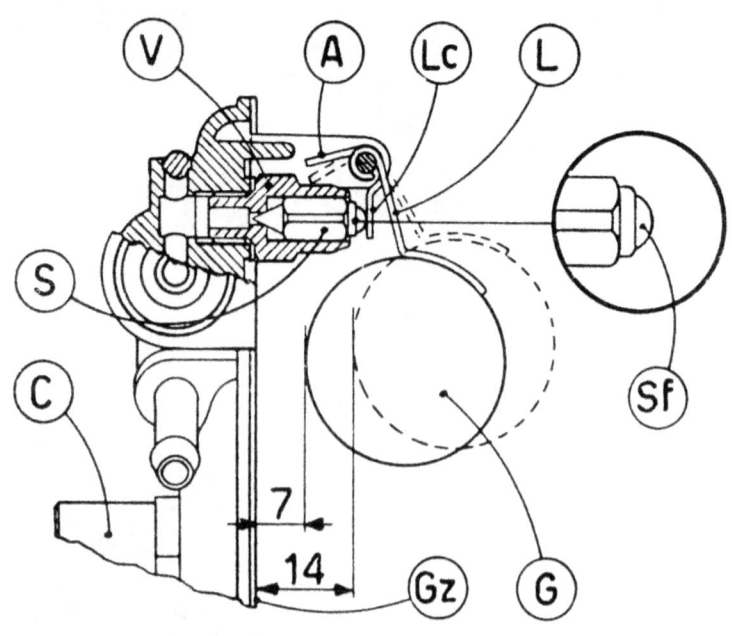

1. Make sure that the needle valve (V) is screwed well down in its seat.
2. Hold the carburetor cover (C) in a vertical position as the weight of the float (G) would otherwise lower the mobile sphere (Sf) mounted on the needle (S).
3. With the carburetor cover (C) vertical and the tab (Lc) of the float lightly touching the sphere "X" mm from the cover with the gasket (Gz) mounted and closely adhering to it.
4. After levelling, check that the stroke of the float (G) is "Z" mm; if not, modify the position of tab (A).
5. Should the float (G) not be correctly placed, modify the position of the tabs (L) of the float until they reach the required point, taking care that the tab (Lc) is perpendicular to the needle axis (S) and that it does not have any indentations which might affect the free movement of the needle itself.
6. Check that the float (G) turns freely on its fulcrum.

NOTE:

Should it be necessary to change needle valve (V), the new valve must be securely screwed down into place, using a new seal, and the levelling operations repeated.

Disassembly and re-assembly of two typical models will be given here. The procedures can be applied to other carburetors of the same configuration with minor, obvious differences.

> As noted in the index, certain of the carburetor models discussed here are also fitted to other automobile makes. Some minor differences in mounting and linkage prevail, but all maintenance and adjustment data given here can be applied.

WEBER 26 IM - IMB

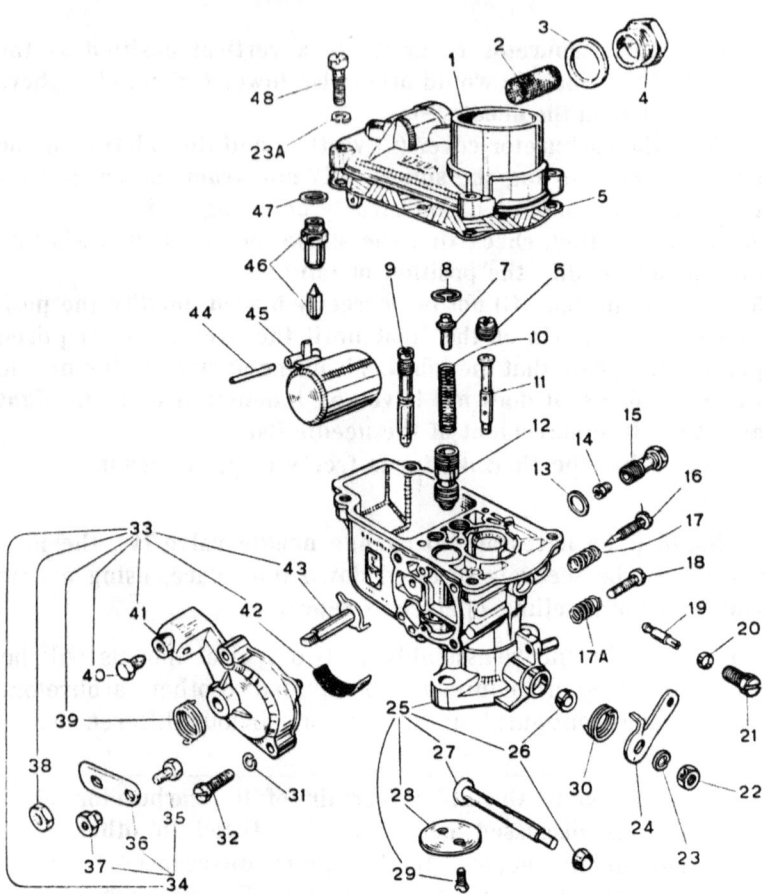

Components of Weber 26 IM carburetter

Key to Fig: 1 Float chamber cover 2 Filter
3 Gasket 4 Filter plug 5 Gasket 6 Vapour well screw and air inlet 7 Spring guide 8 Snap ring
9 Starting jet 10 Spring 11 Vapour well 12 Starting valve
13 Gasket 14 Main jet 15 Main jet holder
16 Idling mixture adjuster 17 Spring 18 Throttle stop
19 Idling jet 20 Gasket 21 Idling jet holder
22 Nut 23 Lockwashers 24 Throttle control lever
25 Body 26 Shaft seal 27 Throttle shaft
28 Butterfly valve 29 Screws 30 Spring 31 Lockwasher
32 Screw 33 Starting lever assembly 34 Valve lever assembly 35 Screw 36 Valve lever 37 Nut
38 Lever-to-shaft retaining nut 39 Spring 40 Setscrew
41 Bowden wire grip 42 Filter (22 IM only) 43 Valve shaft
44 Float pivot 45 Float, brass or nylon 46 Fuel inlet valve 47 Gasket 48 Float chamber cover retaining screw

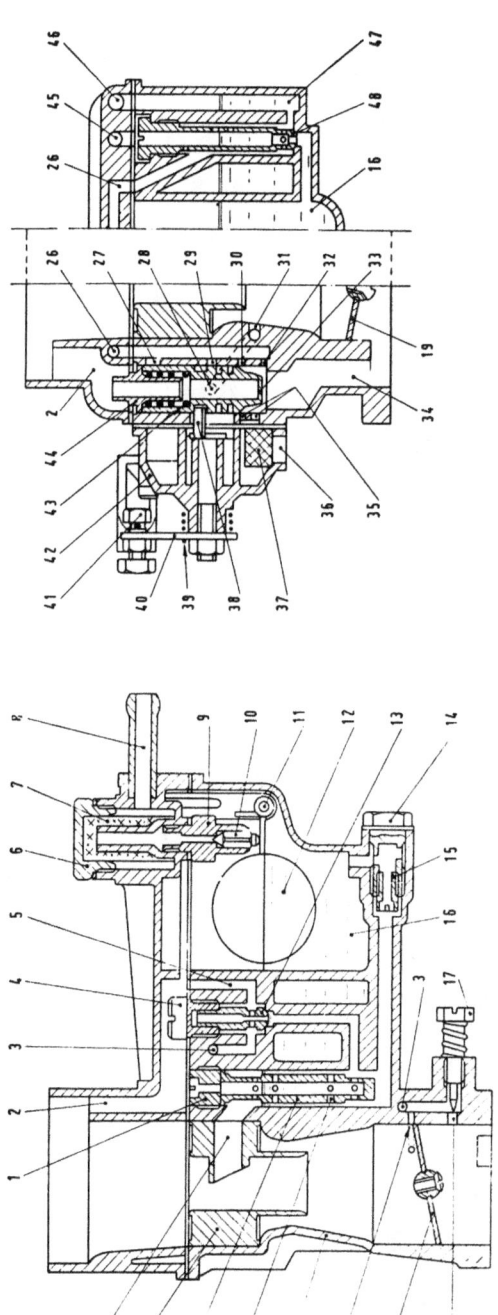

Sections through Weber 22 IM and 26 IM carburetters

Key to Fig: 1 Air inlet to vapour well 2 Air intake 3 Idling mixing duct 4 Idling jet holder 5 Idling air intake 6 Filter plug 7 Filter 8 Fuel inlet pipe 9 Fuel inlet valve 10 Valve needle 11 Float pivot 12 Float 13 Idling jet 14 Main jet holder 15 Main jet 16 Float chamber 17 Idling adjustment 18 Variable jet 19 Butterfly valve 20 Bypass 21 Venturi 22 Fuel vapour outlets 23 Fuel vapour well 24 Throat 25 Spray nozzle 26 Enriched vapour duct 27 Air dilution inlet 28 Transition duct 29 and 30 Enriched vapour inlets 31 Transition duct outlet 32 Enriched vapour inlet 33 Starting valve 34 Starting mixture duct 35 Dilution air ports 36 Dilution air intake (22 IM only) 37 Air filter (22 IM only) 38 Valve lifter 39 Lever spring 40 Valve lever 41 Control wire termination 42 Cover 43 Valve spring 44 Spring guide 45 Starting jet air supply 46 Reserve well air supply 47 Starting reserve well 48 Starting jet

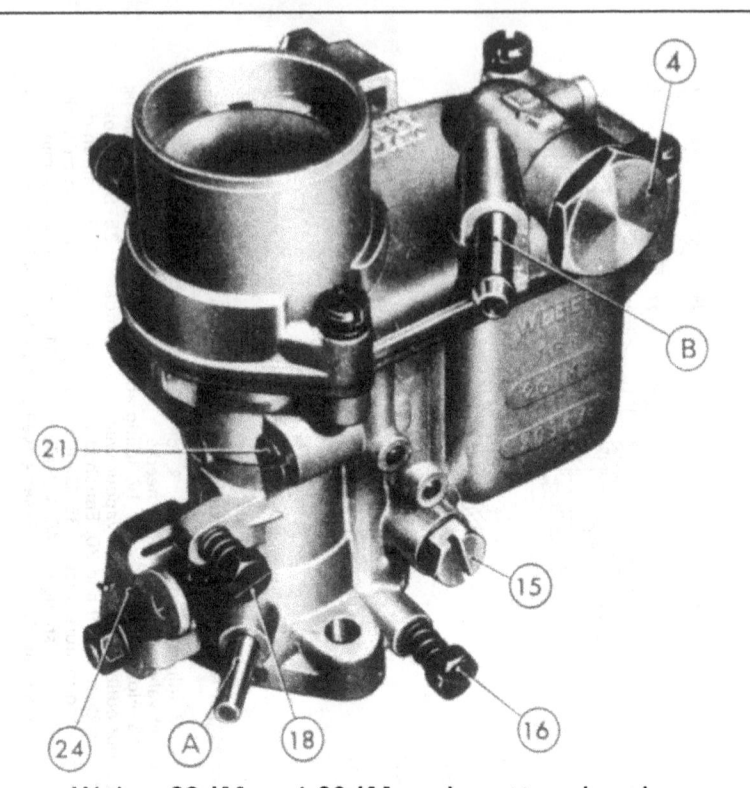

Weber 22 IM and 26 IM carburetter showing main adjustments

Key to Fig: **A** Vacuum advance line connection
B Fuel line connection   4 Filter plug   15 Main jet holder
16 Idling mixture adjuster   18 Throttle stop   21 Idling jet holder   24 Throttle control lever

REMOVAL
1. Remove the air filter assembly.
2. Disconnect the fuel feed line from carburetor.
3. Remove the throttle and choke control.
4. Remove the nuts and washers which secure the flange to the manifold.
5. Lift the carburetor vertically, being careful not to let foreign matter into the manifold.

DISASSEMBLY AND ASSEMBLY
Fuel Filter
1. Remove the fuel filter by unscrewing the cap **1**, the gasket **2** and the strainer **3**.
2. Clean the parts in fuel and dry with compressed air.

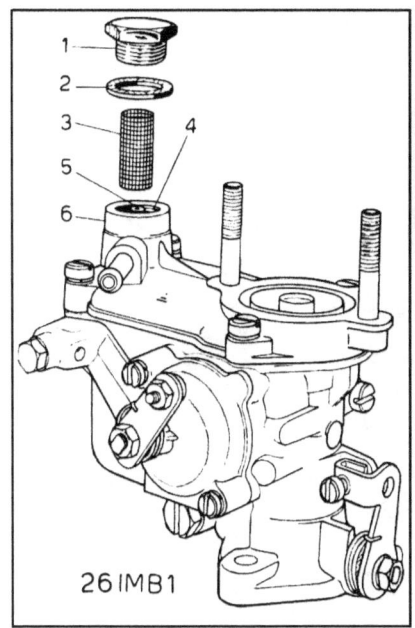 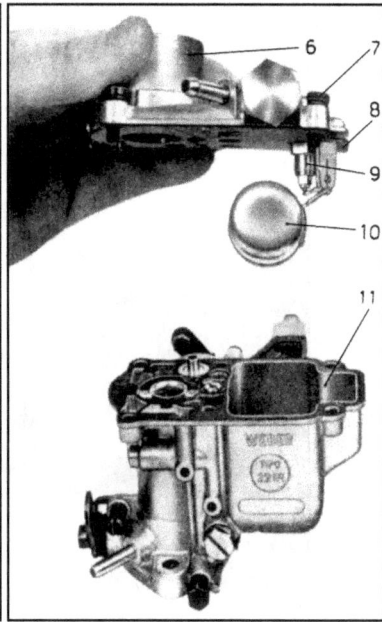

Carburetor Cover
1. Remove four cover screws.
2. Lift cover off, keeping it parallel to carburetor body, taking care not to displace gasket **8** which must adhere to the cover and not to damage float **10**. After removal place the cover in an upside-down position.
3. Slide the float fulcrum pin **15** from its seat by pushing with a small diameter pin from the spring slot support side and withdraw with pliers.
4. Disassemble the needle valve using a 10 mm box wrench, taking care that the needle **14** remains in the valve seat **9** to avoid damage.
5. Remove gaskets.
6. Assemble in reverse order.
7. Set float level.

Main Jet
1. Unscrew jetholder **20** with a 10 mm wrench.
2. Unscrew the main jet **22** from the jetholder **20** with an ordinary screwdriver. It is convenient, whenever it is not being replaced because of deformations, to leave the gasket **21** in the jetholder **20**.
3. Carry out the cleaning and rinsing operations with clean fuel and blow out with compressed air, being careful to avoid the use of metal points for cleaning the calibrated orifices.

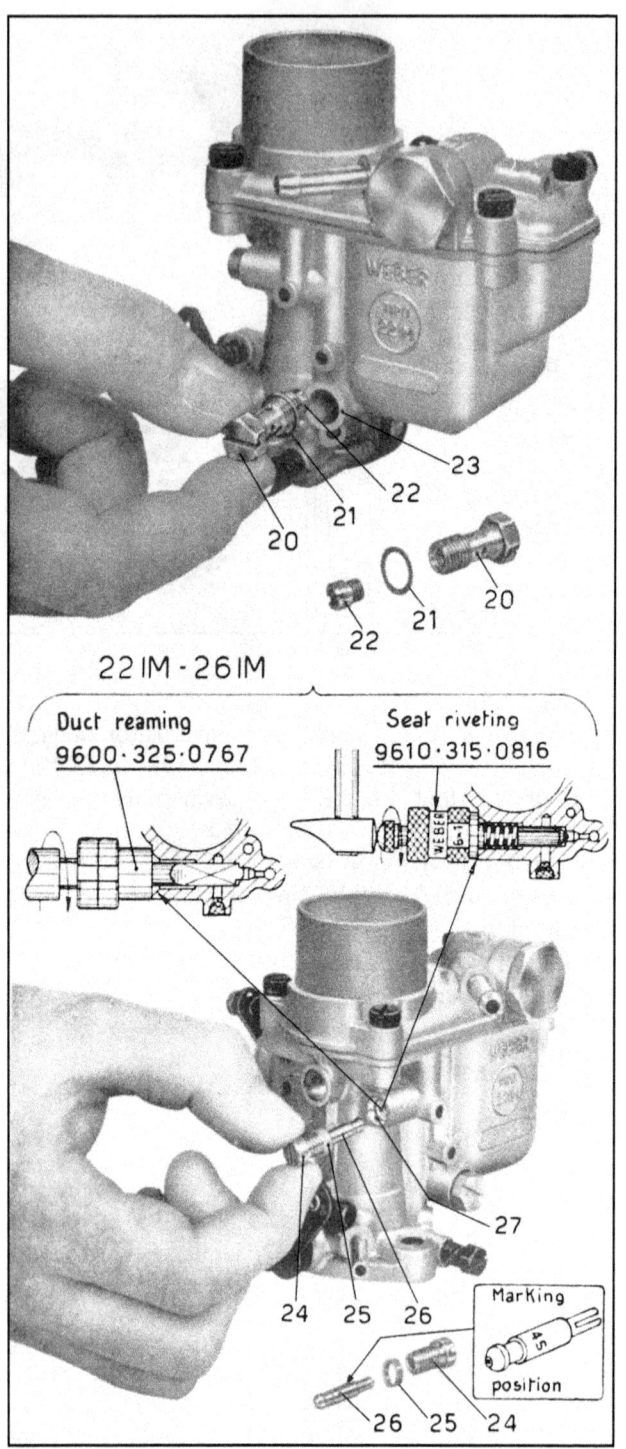

Idling Jet
1. Unscrew the jetholder **24**.
2. Slide out the idling jet **26**, inserted in the jetholder **24** by means of a bayonet joint.
3. Slide out the sealing ring **25** and then proceed to clean the disassembled parts carefully noting that the sealing ring **25** is in perfect condition. Make any necessary replacements.

Emulsion Tube — Air Corrector Jet
1. Unscrew air corrector jet **29**.
2. Remove the emulsion tube **28** from its seat in the body of the carburetor.
3. Carefully clean the tube **28** and its seat **30** in the carburetor body: avoid using metal points.
4. Clean the air corrector jet **29** with fuel and compressed air, avoiding the use of metal points.

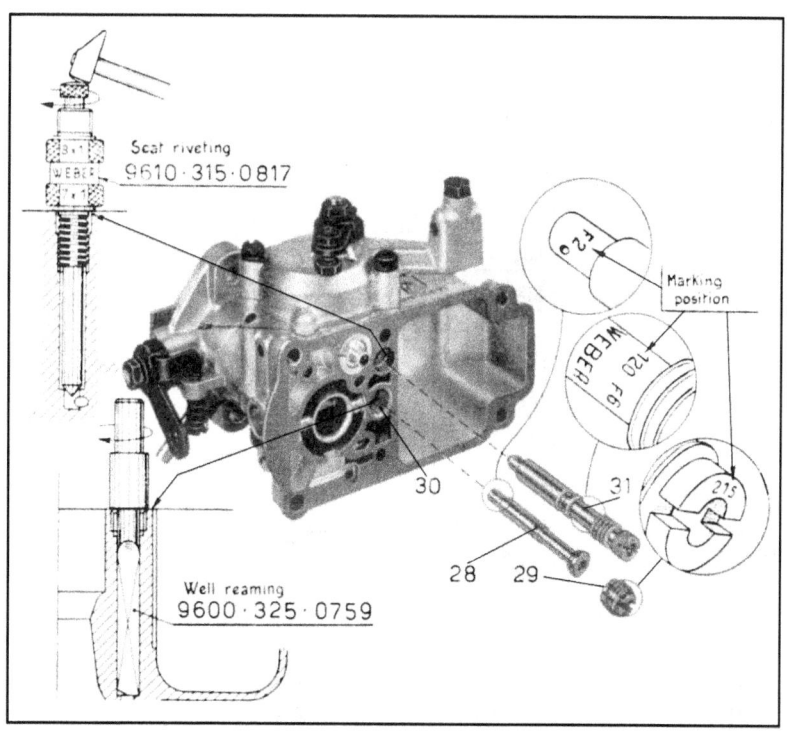

Pipe Inspection

Avoid using inappropriate tools in the fuel pipes since their size is important to the functioning of the carburetor and have been establshed to give best conditions possible.

It is, therefore, indispensible that inspection and cleaning of the pipes should be carried out after the various devices making up the carburetor have been completely disassembled.

For inspection of pipes which are obstructed, proceed as follows:
1. Bore out the lead plugs and then, using Weber gauges 9620.175.1846 - 9620.175.1847 - 9620.175.1848 — inspect the block ducts, so eliminating any residue or deposits. Clean the ducts with compressed air.
2. Block the inspected pipes then, using new plugs and beating them with Weber punch 9610.315.0823.
3. Check the perfect seal of the new plugs with fuel. Repeat the riveting operation should the seal not be perfect.

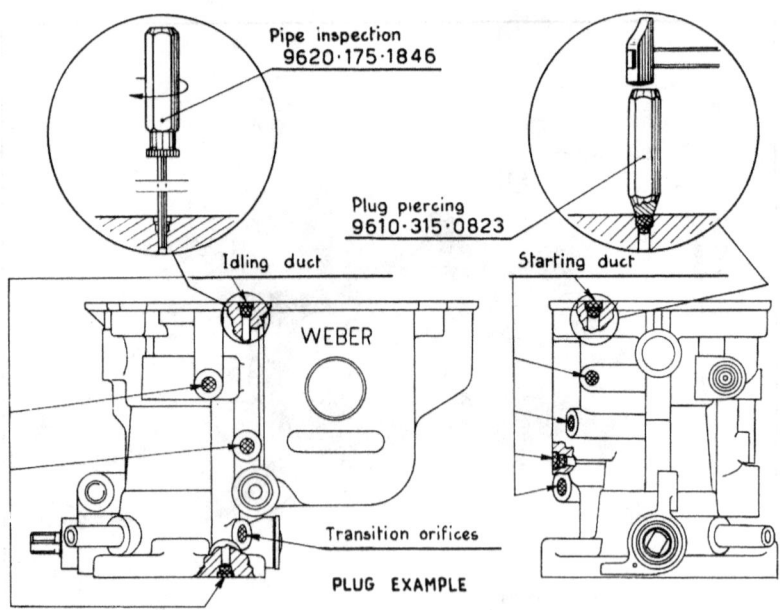

RE-ASSEMBLY
Main Jet

Before re-assembling the main jet **22** on jetholder **20**, check that the calibration orifice corresponds to that punched on the side of the jet itself which must correspond to the adjustment data of the carburetor under examination. Make replacements where necessary.

1. Re-assemble the main jet **22**, carefully tightening it on the jetholder **20** so as to avoid possible leakages of fuel along the threads.
2. Replace the gasket **21** should there be any signs of any defects, however slight.
3. Then proceed to assemble the jetholder **20**, complete with jet **22** and gasket **21**, on the body of the carburetor, carefully tightening it so that the gasket may guarantee a perfect seal with the contact surface **23**.

Idling Jet

Check the calibration of this jet **26** too, as indicated above, ascertaining that the terminal sealing cone functions perfectly, allowing no leakages which would prejudice the carburetor's working.
1. Slide the sealing ring **25** over the jetholder **24** and then reassemble the idling jet **26** on the jetholder **24** making sure that the spring is sufficient to hold the jet fixed on the jetholder. Tighten the jetholder, complete with sealing ring and jet, on to the carburetor body so that the ring **25** adheres to the tapered seat **27** of the idling jet housing duct.

Emulsion Tube — Air Corrector Jet
1. Before placing the emulsion tube **28** in the housing **30** of the carburetor, check that the marking (e.g. F 2) punched on the back of the tube itself corresponds to the adjustment data for the carburetor being examined.
2. Then assemble the air corrector jet **29** after checking the calibration of this too; tighten up the tube **28** then, carefully, so as to fix it firmly in its seat.

When checking calibrated parts it is always advisable to use Weber series of micron plugs 9620.150.0016.

IMPORTANT

When disassembling the calibrated parts (main jet, idling jet, emulsion tube, etc.) great care must be taken to reassemble them correctly, always checking that the calibrated value corroesponds to the adjustment data for the carburetor under examination.

STARTING DEVICE
Disassembling

Carry out the disassembling of the starter device in the following manner:
1. Loosen screws **45** to remove cover sheath support **46**.
2. Unscrew starter jet **31**.

3. Remove stop ring **32** and then withdraw spring guide **33**, spring **34** and the starting valve **35**.

4. Rinse and blow out the disassembled parts, avoiding the use of metal points when inspecting the calibrated orifices.

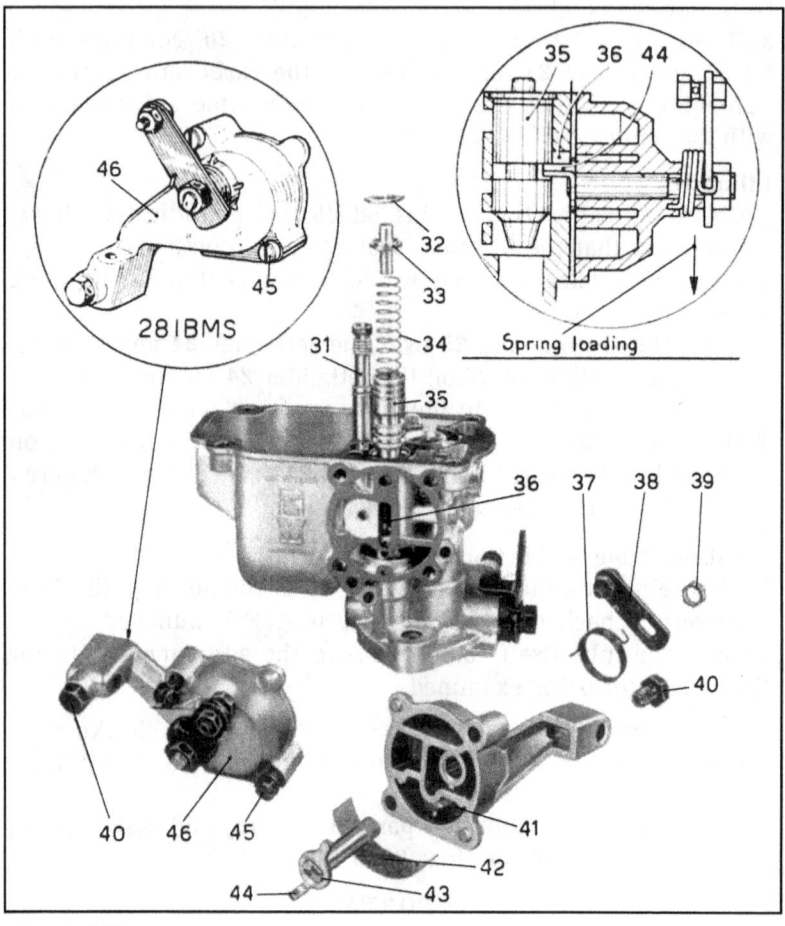

Assembling

For assembling the component parts of the starter device control, observe the placing of the parts in the accompanying illustration, taking care to:

1. Carry out the usual rinsing and blowing with compressed air, being particularly careful with the filter gauze **42**.

2. Anchor the spring **37** to the cover **46** and load it to hook on the lever **38** which, in turn, is locked by nut **39**.

STARTING DEVICE CONTROL
Disassembling

When disassembling the component parts of the starter de-

vice control it is necessary to:
1. Withdraw the filter gauze **42** from its seat **41**.
2. Unscrew the lever **38** fixing nut **39**.
3. Remove the lever **38** and the spring **37**.
4. Unscrew the sheath fixing screw **40**.

STARTING DEVICE
Assembling

Before fixing the device control to the body of the carburetor it is necessary to:
1. Clean the ducts of the starter valve **35** seat and the starter jet **31** thoroughly with fuel and compressed air only.
2. Ensure that the pipes of the starter device are not blocked.
3. Check that the number punched on the jet corresponds to the adjustment data and that the diameter of the axial orifice is the one indicated by the number.
4. Screw in and carefully tighten the starter jet **31**.
5. Insert the starter valve **35**, taking care to check that it may run freely.
6. Place the spring **34** inside the valve **35**.
7. Set the spring guide **33** in place.
8. Replace the stop ring **32** in the groove in the carburetor cover, pressing lightly and making sure that the spring **34** and spring guide **33** are not moved from their seats.

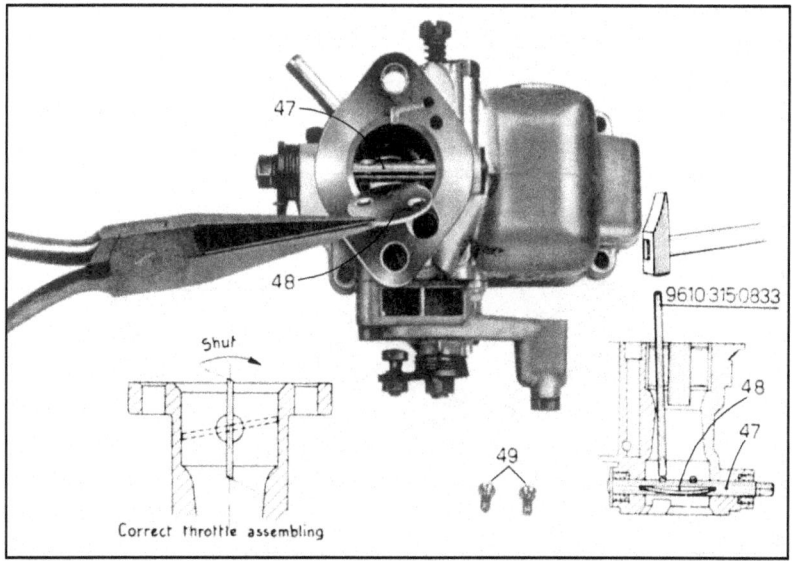

Correct throttle assembling

9. Then assemble the complete device on the carburetor body, taking care that the tab **44** fits into the groove in the valve **35** through the slot **36**.

10. Lock the sheath support cover to the carburetor with fixing screws **45**.

MAIN SPINDLE — THROTTLE VALVE
Disassembling

1. Remove the throttle **48** fixing screws **49**, turn the spindle **47** and, holding it in that position, slide the throttle **48** out with a pair of flat pliers.
2. Unscrew nut **54**.
3. Remove washer **53**, lever **52** and spring **51**.
4. Extract the spindle **47**.
5. Remove the nylon seating rings **50**.

Assembling

Carry out the usual cleaning and checking operations of the disassembled parts.

1. Fit the spindle alone **47** in place in the carburetor, making certain it moves freely. If any resistance is noted, bore out with Weber reamer 9600.035.0409 and replace the spindle with a

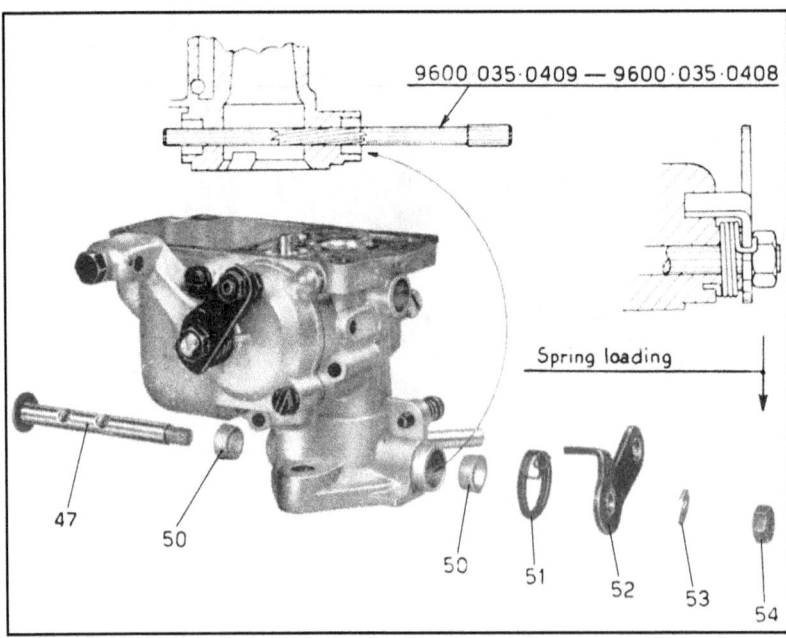

new one.
2. If there is excessive play due to wear, between the spindle and the duct, use a 6.5 mm oversize spindle (increase of 0.5 mm). In this case the duct must be bored to 6.5 mm using Weber reamer 9600.0358.0408, substituting the nylon bushes **50** with others of 6.5 mm.
3. Fit the nylon bushes **50** in their relative seats.
4. Insert spindle **47**, making sure there is no jamming.
5. Anchor the spring **51** to the carburetor body with the special terminal and then insert the lever **52**, washer **53** and screw nut **54** on to the spindle **47**, **but not definitively**.
6. Load spring **51**, hooking the other end to the lever **52**.
7. Tighten nut **54**.
8. Again repeat the spindle movement check as previously indicated.
9. Turn spindle **47** so that the throttle slot is facing upwards. Slide in throttle **48** vertically (with fixing holes parallel to the spindle axis) making sure it is mounted with the bevel edge facing the internal duct wall. When released the throttle valve must settle, perfectly adhering to the duct walls.
10. Insert throttle valve fixing screws **49** in the holes in the spindle **47** lightly screwing them up.
11. Turn the spindle **47** a few times to set the throttle valve **48**, and then tighten up the fixing screws **49**.
12. Using the special Weber 9610.315.0833 punch, beat screws **49**, taking care not to deform the throttle spindle.
13. Check, by turning the spindle completely, that the throttle valve is completely open and centered with the duct center line.

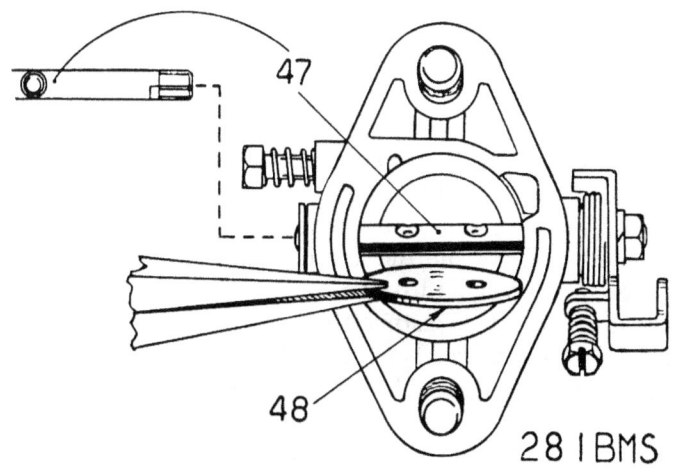

INSTALLING CARBURETOR ON ENGINE

After completing the maintenance operations on the carburetor, it may be installed on the engine by following the general directions given below:

1. Ensure that the gaskets, or seals, between the manifold and the carburetor are in good condition. It is always advisable to use new seals, especially when mounting overhauled carburetors. Do not use any adhesives.

2. Fit the washers and carburetor nuts, tightening them uniformly so as to avoid deformation or possible breakage of the flange.

3. Connect the accelerator control, which must work normally in order to permit both complete opening of the throttle valve by pressing down the accelerator pedal completely and returning to the closed position when pedal is released. No friction or resistance to movement must be noted during this movement.

4. When connecting the starting device cable, make sure it runs the full course; make several preliminary trials before starting engine.

The starter device valve must be completely raised from its seat when starting and return within its seat when the starting device is excluded; check that the cable does not remain taut, since, otherwise, the oscillations of the engine would cause the valve to open.

ENGINE STARTING AND SLOW RUNNING ADJUSTMENT

Before starting the engine it is advisable to carry out a first, approximate, adjustment of the mixture adjustment screws **56** and idle running **55**; the definite adjustment will then be found after the engine is running.

Carry out the following:

1. Mixture adjustment screw **56** must be loosened ¾ turn from the fully closed position.

2. The running adjustment screw **55** must be given 1 full turn from the point when the resistance of lever tab **52** is felt, so that the throttle valve is slightly open.

3. Idle adjustment must be carried out through the running adjustment screw **55** and the idle mixture adjustment screw **56**. The screw **55** allows adjustment of the throttle opening; screw **56** has the task of adjusting the quantity of mixture coming from the idle duct, which mixes with the air drawn in by the engine, so making it possible to obtain the best mixture strength for normal idle. The idle adjustment must be done when the engine is hot and running, by first adjusting the idle opening of

the throttle through screw **55**.

Acting on screw **56**, the mixture which will give the fastest and most stable running for that throttle opening is found; the throttle minimum opening is reduced to the most suitable idling speed, re-checking the mixture through screw **56**.

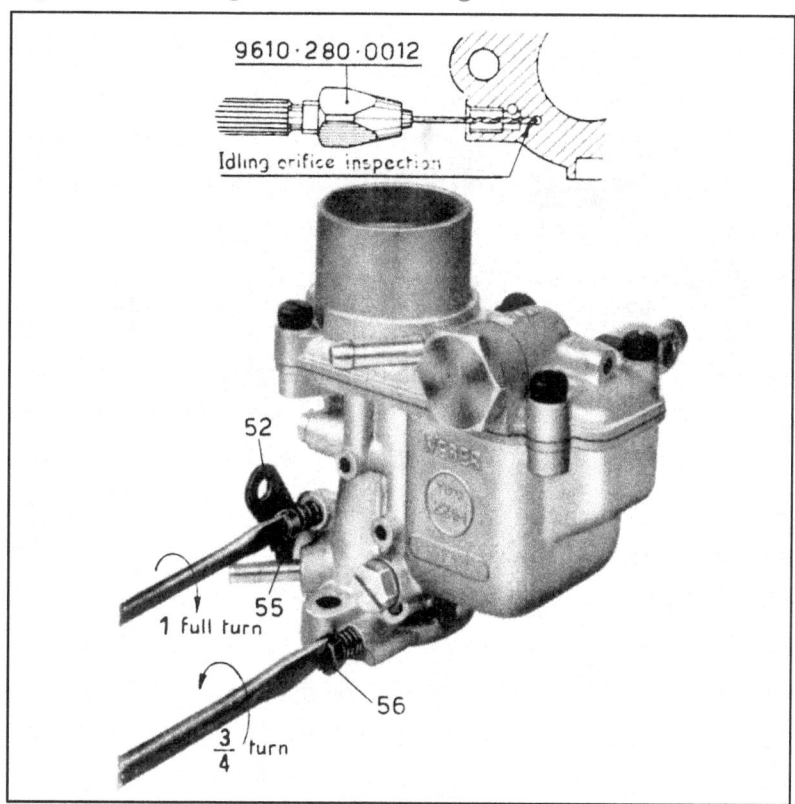

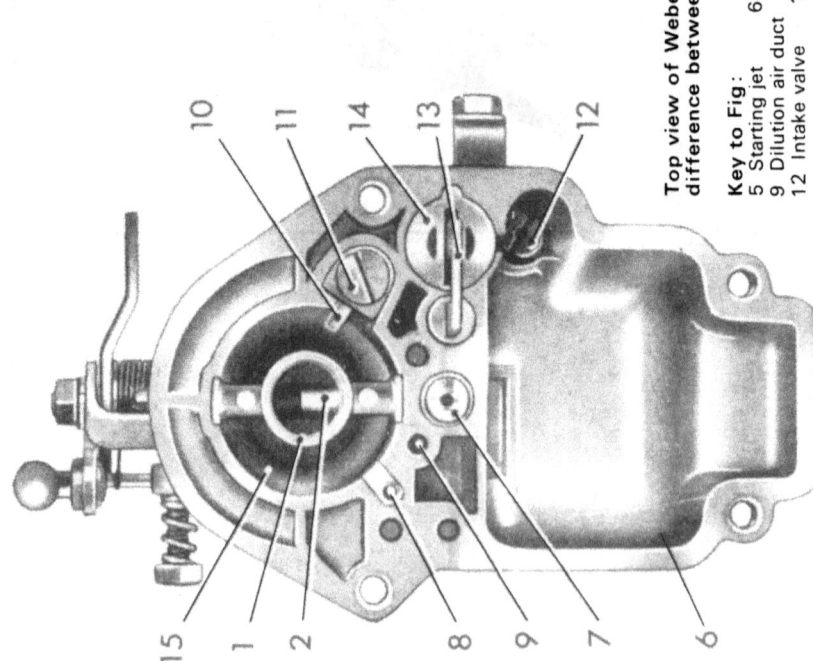

Top view of Weber carburetters, float chamber cover removed, to show difference between the 22/26 IM (right) and 28 ICP (left) models

Key to Fig: 1 Throat   2 Spray nozzle   3 and 4 Spring guide and snap ring
5 Starting jet   6 Float chamber   7 Vapour well and air inlet   8 Idling speed bush
9 Dilution air duct   10 Acceleration pump jet   11 Delivery valve
12 Intake valve   13 Pump control rod   14 Pump spring retaining plate   15 Venturi

Weber 26 IM carburetter installed on engine

Key to Fig: 1 Throttle control cable 2 Relay lever
3 Cable retaining screw 4 Throttle cable clamp
5 Throttle control rod 7 Throttle control lever 8 Throttle stop 9 Idling jet holder 10 Main jet holder
11 Idling mixture adjuster 12 Choke control cable
13 Choke control lever 14 Fuel line from fuel pump
15 Filter plug 16 Fuel overflow tray and drain
17 Manifold to carburetter adapter 18 Vacuum advance line

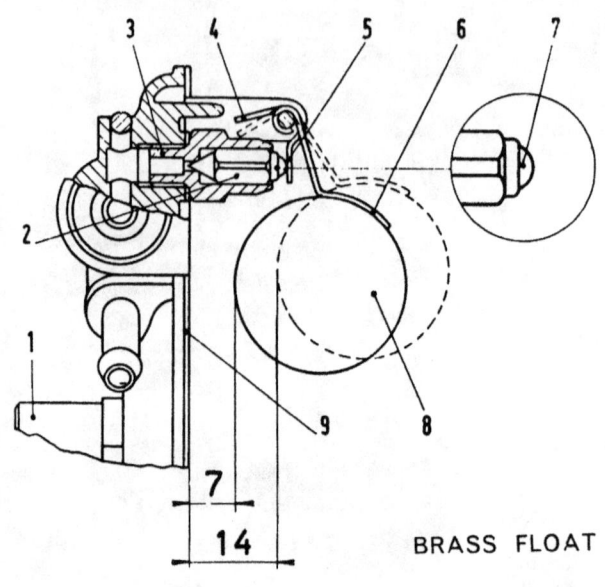

BRASS FLOAT

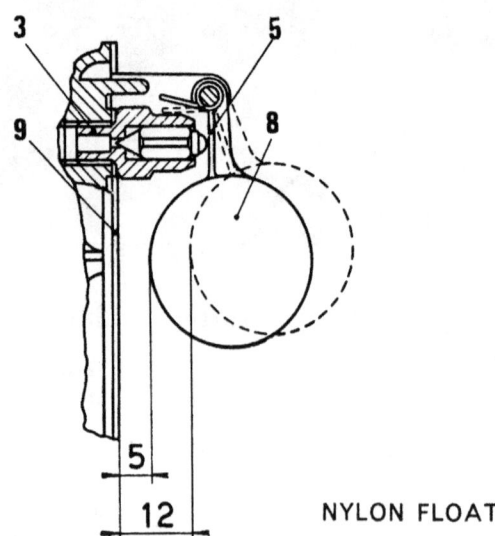

NYLON FLOAT

Float adjustment 22 IM and 26 IM carburetters

Key to Fig:
1 Float chamber cover   2 Needle
3 Needle valve   4 Lug   5 Valve contact face
6 Float arm   7 Detail of needle valve   8 Float
9 Gasket

WEBER 28 ICP

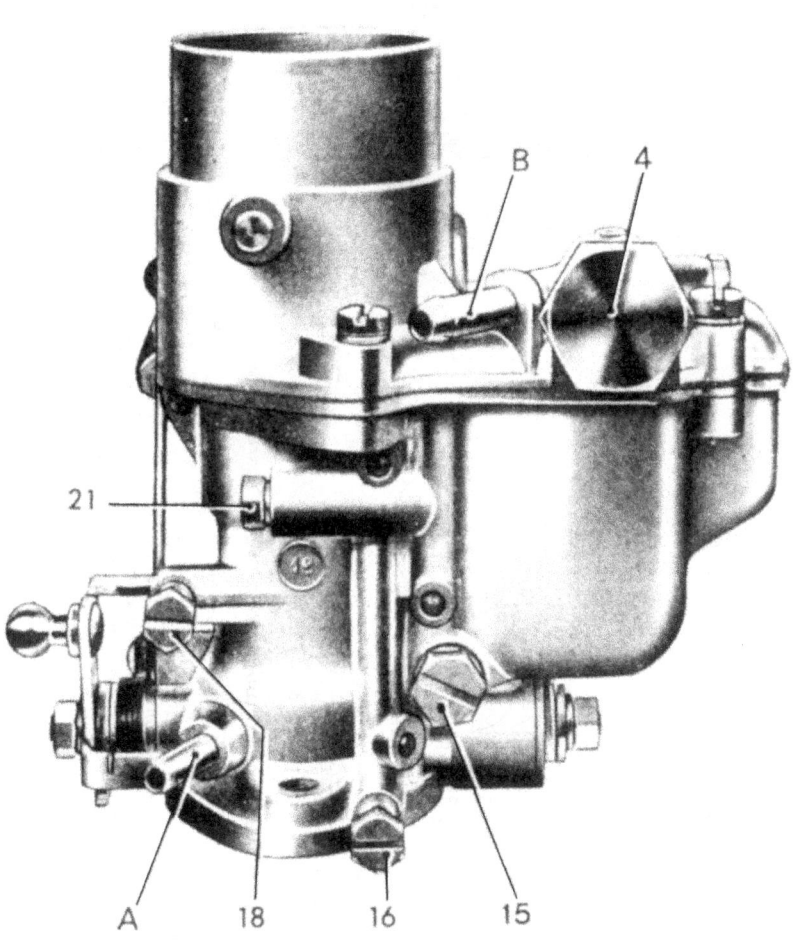

Weber 28 ICP carburetter showing main controls

Key to Fig:
A Vacuum advance line connection
B Fuel line connection 4 Filter plug 16 Idling mixture adjuster 18 Throttle stop 21 Idling jet holder

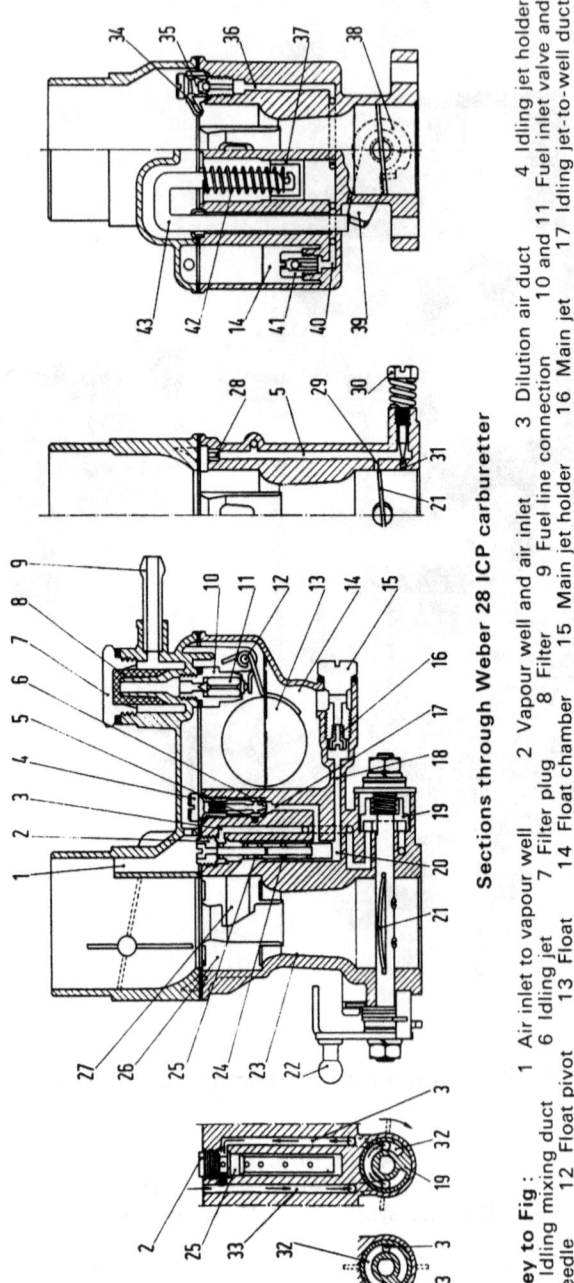

Sections through Weber 28 ICP carburetter

Key to Fig: 1 Air inlet to vapour well 2 Vapour well and air inlet 3 Dilution air duct 4 Idling jet holder 5 Idling mixing duct 6 Idling jet 7 Filter plug 8 Filter 9 Fuel line connection 10 and 11 Fuel inlet valve and needle 12 Float pivot 13 Float 14 Float chamber 15 Main jet holder 16 Main jet 17 Idling jet-to-well duct 18 Main jet-to-well duct 19 Vapour dilution diaphragm 20 Vapour well sump 21 Butterfly valve 22 Throttle lever 23 Venturi 24 Enriched vapour inlets 25 Enriched vapour diaphragm 26 Throat 27 Spray nozzle 28 Idling speed bush 29 By-pass 30 Idling adjustment 31 Variable jet 32 Dilution duct diaphragm 33 Dilution duct extension 34 Acceleration pump jet 35 Delivery valve 36 Delivery duct 37 Pump piston 38 Pump lever 39 Idling lever 40 Pump intake duct 41 Intake valve 42 Pump spring 43 Pump control rod

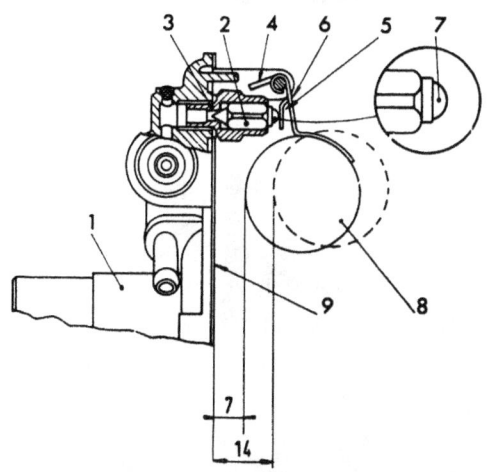

Float adjustment 28 ICP carburetters

Key to Fig:
3 Needle valve
6 Float arm
9 Gasket

1 Float chamber cover
4 Lug
7 Detail of needle valve

2 Needle
5 Valve contact face
8 Float

WEBER 32.IMPE.4

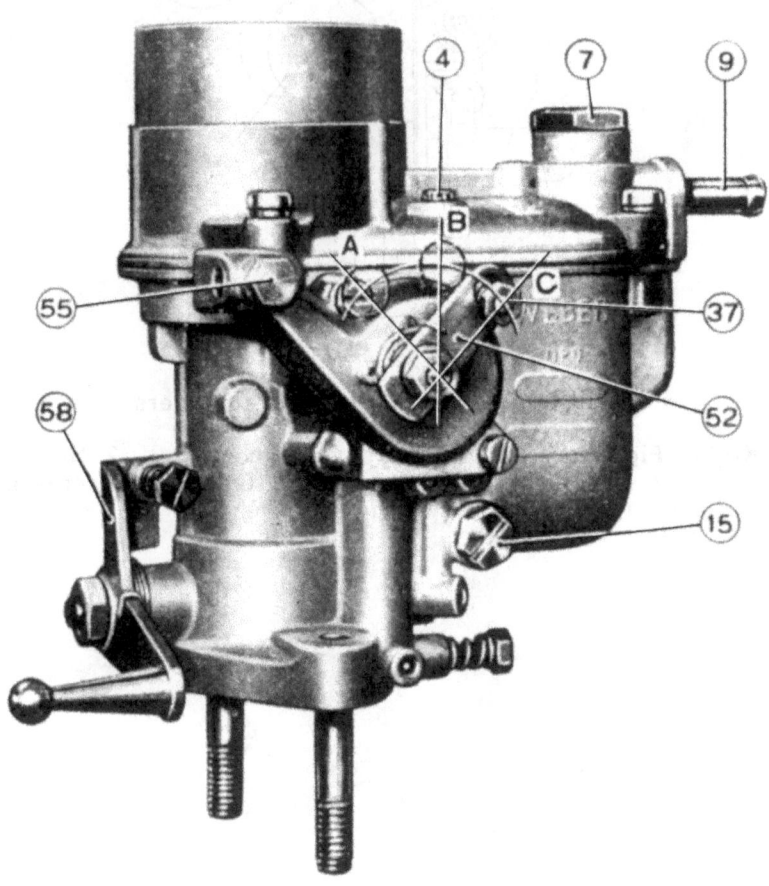

32.IMPE.4 Starting lever positions and location of jets

Key to Fig:
4 Idling jet holder
7 Filter cover
9 Fuel inlet connection device bowden screw
15 Main jet holder
37 Starting device bowden screw
52 Starting device control lever
55 Bowden fixing screw
58 Throttle control lever

Starting device lever positions: **A** Fully open **B** Half open **C** Closed

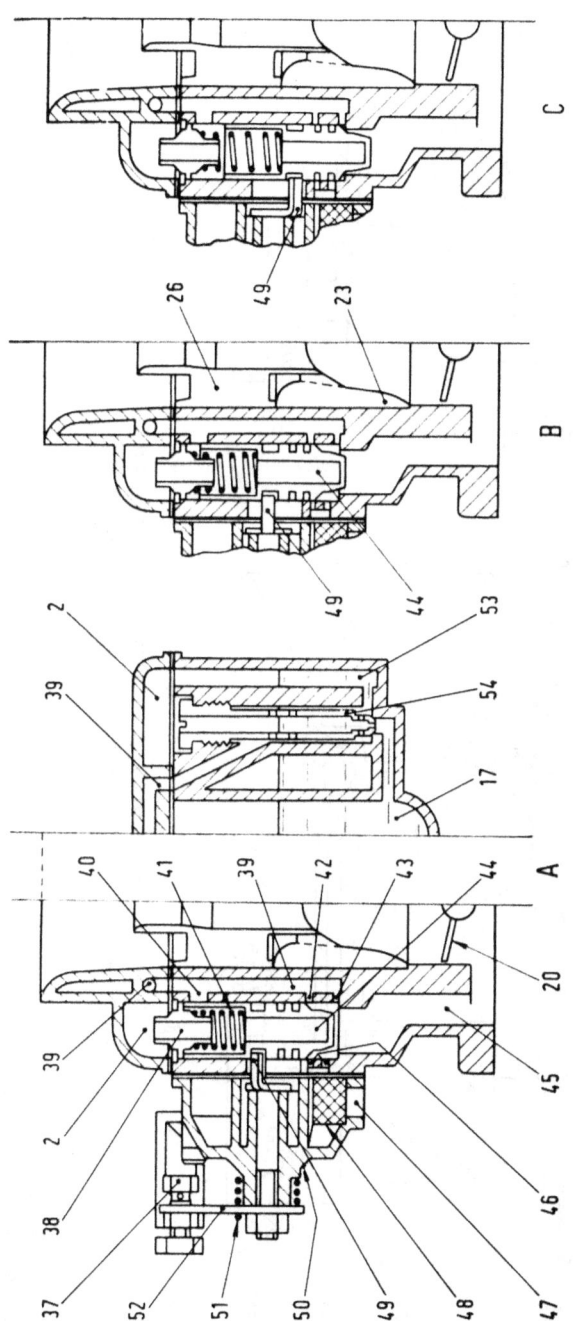

Cutaway diagram of the Weber 32.IMPE.4 starting device

Key to Fig: 2 Air duct 17 Fuel bowl 20 Throttle 23 Venturi 26 Secondary Venturi 37 Starting device bowden screw 38 Hollow spring guide 39 Duct from jet to valve 40 Air hole 42-43 Mixture holes 44 Valve 45 Mixture duct from starting device to main throat 46 Air inlet holes 47 Air inlet slots 48 Air strainer 49 Valve rocker 50 Cover 51 Lever spring 52 Control lever 53 Reserve well 54 Starting jet
Starting device positions: **A** Fully open **B** Half open **C** Closed

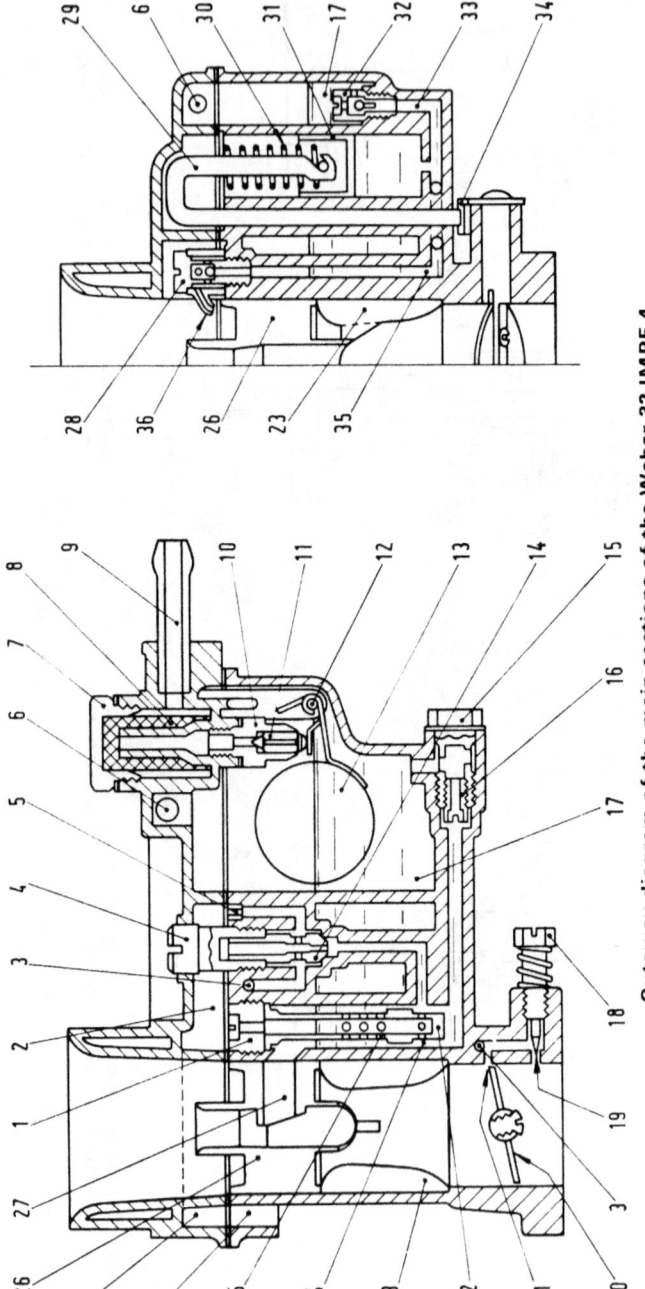

Cutaway diagram of the main sections of the Weber 32.IMPE.4

Key to Fig: 1 Air corrector jet 2 Air intakes 3 Mixture duct to progression and idling holes 4 Idling jet holder 5 Idling air jet 6 Accelerating pump air intake 7 Filter cover 8 Strainer 9 Fuel inlet connection 10 Needle valve seat 11 Valve needle 12 Float pivot 13 Float 14 Idling jet 15 Main jet holder 16 Main jet 17 Bowl 18 Idling adjusting screw 19 Idling hole 20 Throttle 21 Progression hole 22 Emulsioning tube 23 Venturi 24 Emulsioning tube recess 25 Emulsioning holes 26 Secondary Venturi 27 Nozzle 28 Pump delivery valve 29 Pump control rod 30 Spring 31 Accelerating pump plunger 32 Pump inlet valve 33 Pump delivery duct 34 Pump control rod lever 35 Pump valve duct 36 Accelerating pump jet

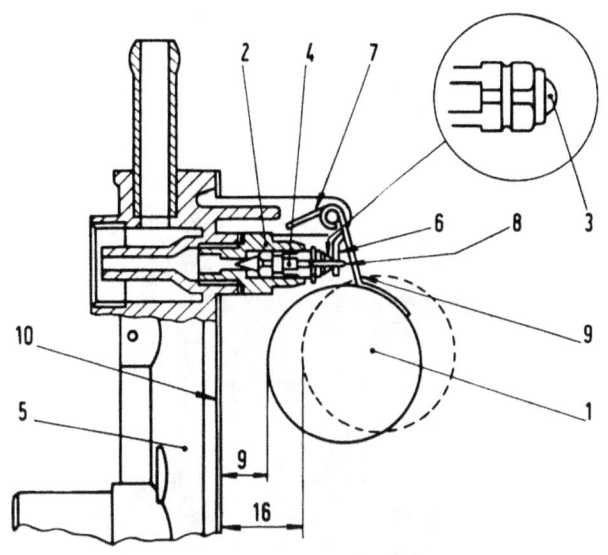

Float adjustment for the Weber 32.IMPE.4

Key to Fig: 1 Float   2 Valve seat   3 Ball   4 Valve needle   5 Carburetter cover   6 Plate   7 Lug   8 Needle hook   9 Float arm   10 Gasket

WEBER 34 DAS & 36 DCD

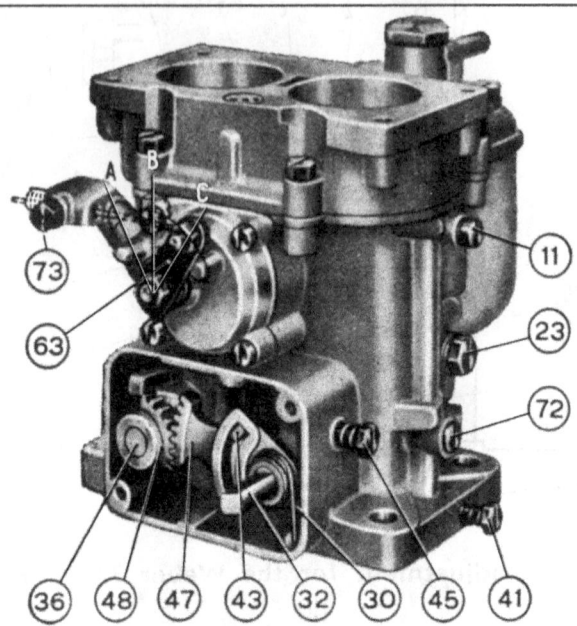

Starting lever positions and location of jets on the Weber 36 DCD 3

Key to Fig: 11 Idling jet 23 Main jets 30 Secondary throttle return spring 32 Primary shaft 36 Secondary shaft 41 Idling mixture adjusting screw 43 Lug 45 Idling speed adjusting screw 47 Primary toothed sector 48 Secondary toothed sector 63 Starting device control lever 72 Progression holes inspection screw 73 Bowden sheath screw **A** Starting device completely inserted **B** Starting device partially inserted **C** Starting device completely released

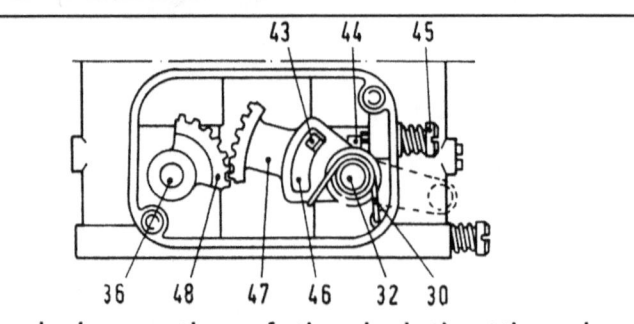

Mechanical operation of the dual throttle valves
See Cutaway Diagram of 36.DCD.3 for Key

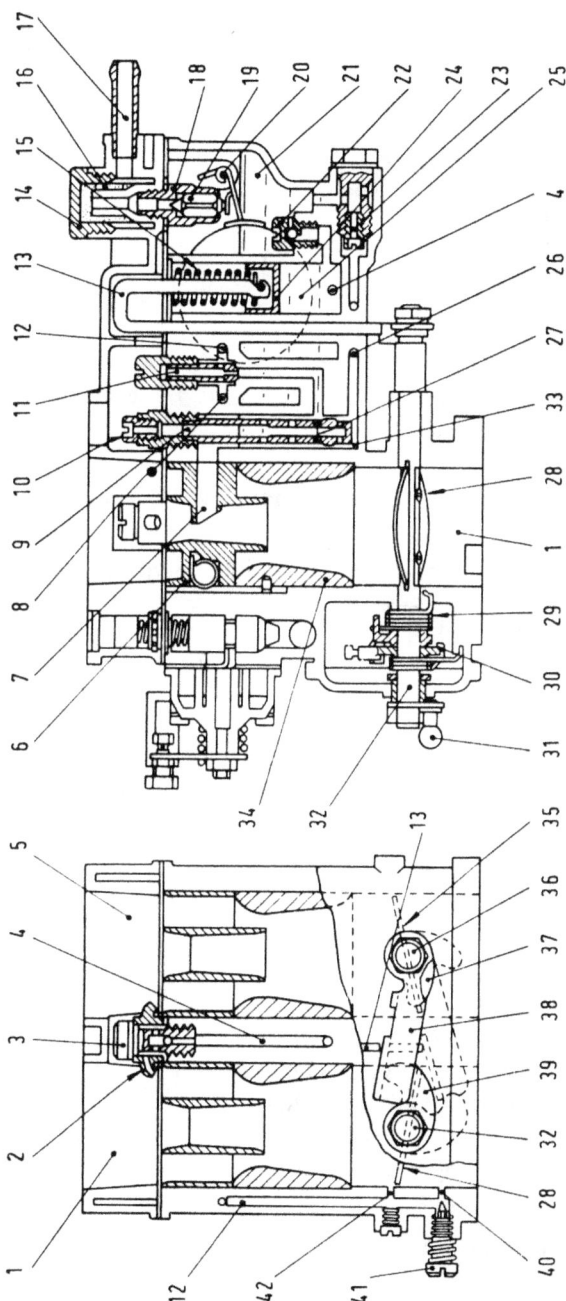

Cutaway diagram of the Weber 36. DCD.3

Key to Fig: 1 Primary intake pipe 2 Pump jet 3 Pump delivery valve 4 Pump delivery duct 5 Secondary intake pipe 6 Auxiliary Venturis 7 Nozzles 8 Idling air orifice 9 Emulsioning tubes 10 Air corrector screw 11 Idling jet 12 Idling mixture duct 13 Pump control rod 14 Strainer 15 Pumping stroke lengthening spring 16 Filter cover 17 Fuel inlet connection 18 Needle valve seat 19 Needle valve 20 Float pivot 21 Bowl 22 Pump inlet valve with discharge orifice 23 Main jets 24 Pump plunger 25 Float 26 Jets-emulsioning tube ducts 27 Emulsioning holes 28 Primary throttle 29 Primary throttle return spring 30 Secondary throttle return spring 31 Throttles main control lever 32 Primary shaft 33 Emulsioning tube recess 34 Primary Venturis 35 Secondary throttle 36 Secondary shaft 37 Secondary pump control lever 38 Pump control lever 39 Primary pump control lever 40 Idling hole to the intake pipe 41 Idling mixture adjusting screw 42 Progression hole 43 Lug 44 Stop sector 45 Idling adjusting screw 46 Primary sector slot 47 Primary toothed sector 48 Secondary toothed sector

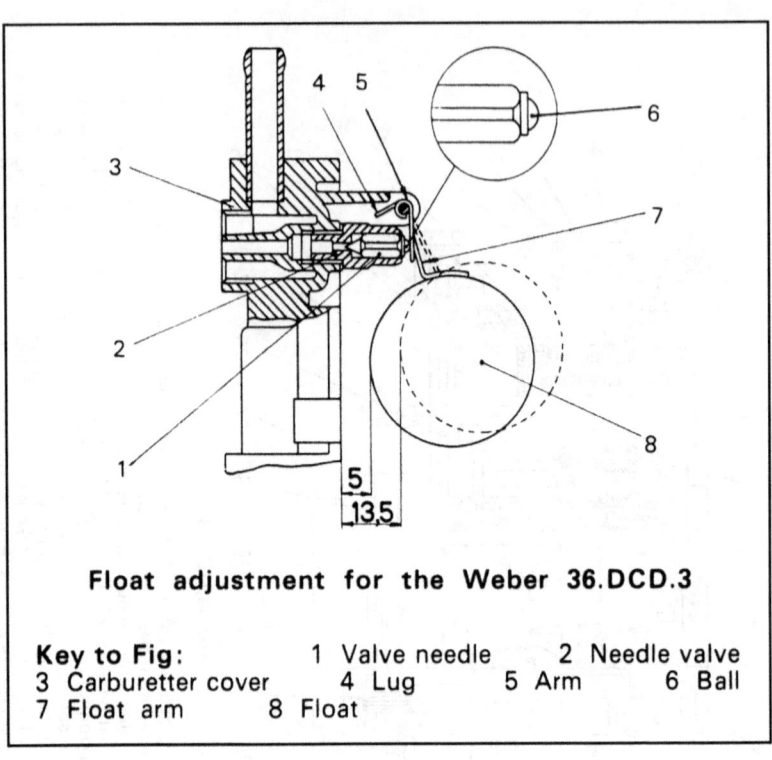

Float adjustment for the Weber 36.DCD.3

Key to Fig: 1 Valve needle   2 Needle valve
3 Carburetter cover   4 Lug   5 Arm   6 Ball
7 Float arm   8 Float

WEBER 34 DAS & 36 DCD

REMOVAL
1. Remove air cleaner assembly.
2. Disconnect fuel line at carburetor.
3. Disconnect automatic choke pipe or choke cable.
4. Disconnect automatic spark advance lead.
5. Disengage the throttle control rod.
6. Remove the flange nuts (Special 14 mm wrench 9650.120.0053 is required for DCD).

DISASSEMBLY AND ASSEMBLY
Fuel Filter
1. Unscrew the cap.
2. Remove gasket and filter screen.

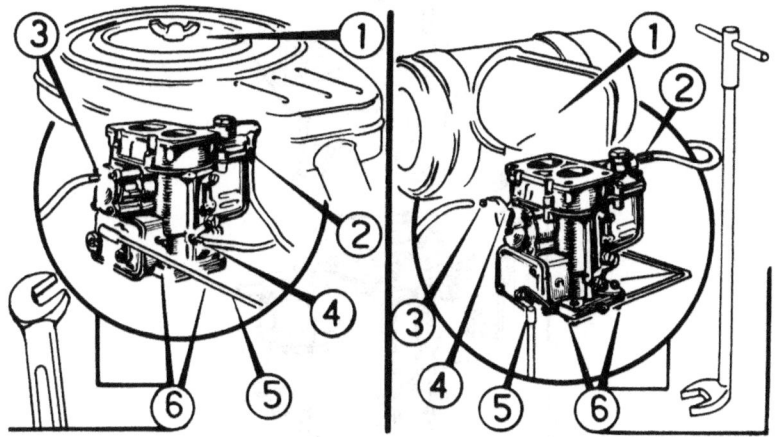

3. Clean screen in fuel and dry with compressed air. Make sure that there is no foreign matter in the filter cavity.
4. Inspect the gasket.
5. Replace filter screen, gasket and cap.

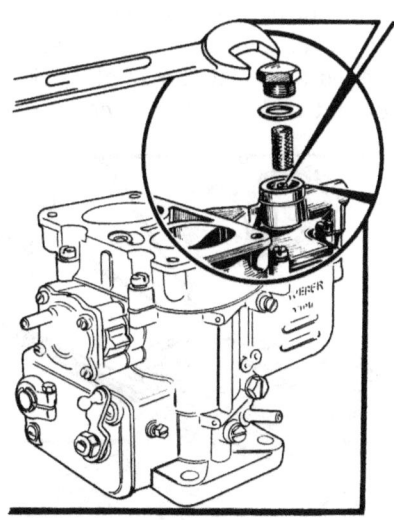

Carburetor Cover
1. Remove cover screws.
2. Lift cover vertically, taking care not to damage float.
3. Inspect gasket.
4. Place cover in inverted position on bench.

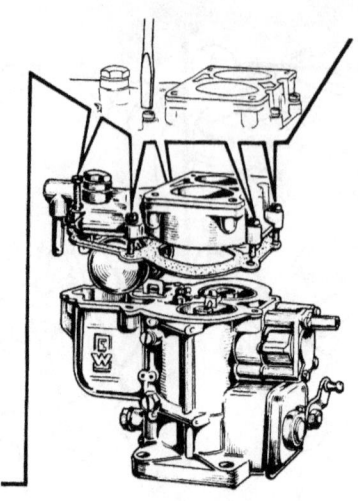

Float & Needle Valve
1. Push the fulcrum pin out from the slotted support side with a small diameter pin and withdraw with pliers.
2. Unscrew the needle valve with a 10 mm box wrench taking care that the needle valve remains in the valve seat to avoid damage.
3. Clean the carburetor orifices with compressed air.
4. Reassemble in reverse order, making sure that the needle valve is not damaged and that the small gasket is sound.
5. Set float level and make sure it is centered in the chamber.

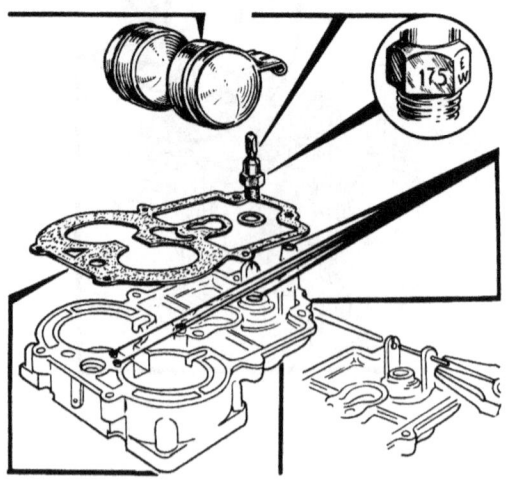

NOTE:
   The weight of the float is critical. If it is leaking, replace it rather than repairing by soldering.

Starter Piston

The starter piston is driven out by using a **non-metallic** punch as shown in the illustration.

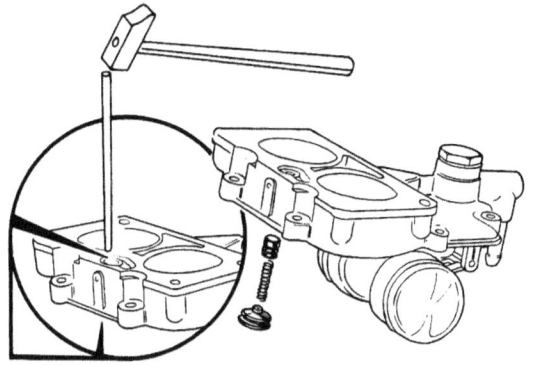

Main Jets
1. Remove the jet holders from the positions shown in the illustration. It will be found that Weber tool 9650.150.0083 (T handle wrench) will be helpful.
2. Remove the jets with a screwdriver as shown.
3. Clean in fuel and blow out with compressed air. Do not push wire or sharp tools through jets.
4. Reinstall in reverse order, taking care that jet holders are tightened securely but not over-tightened.

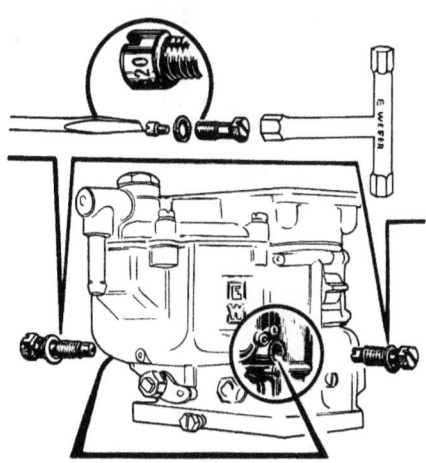

Idling Jets
NOTE: DCD carburetors have only one idling jet.
1. Unscrew jet holders and separate jets. (See illustration)
2. Clean jets in fuel and blow out with compressed air.
3. Clean orifices indicated with compressed air.

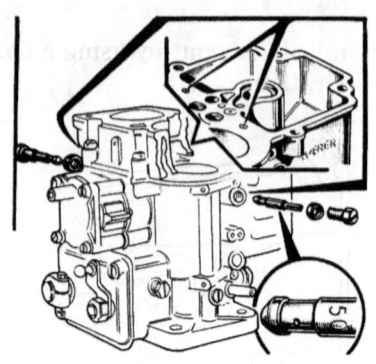

4. Re-install.

NOTE:

If jet wells and seats are corroded, they can be reamed and riveted with special Weber tools as shown in the illustration.

Air Correction Jets & Emulsion Tubes

These are withdrawn vertically as shown. Clean in fuel and blow out with compressed air. Clean the wells in the same fashion.

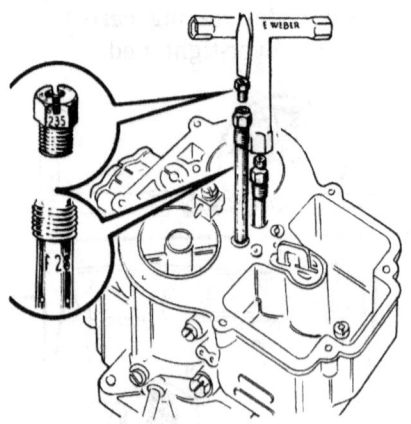

Accelerating Pump
1. Unscrew the pump jet from the housing.
2. Disconnect the pump linkage from the throttle shaft.
3. Lift the pump assembly with a pair of pliers.
4. Clean all parts in fuel and dry with compressed air.
5. Reassemble in reverse order, taking care to make sure that the pump operates freely when the throttle shaft is worked.

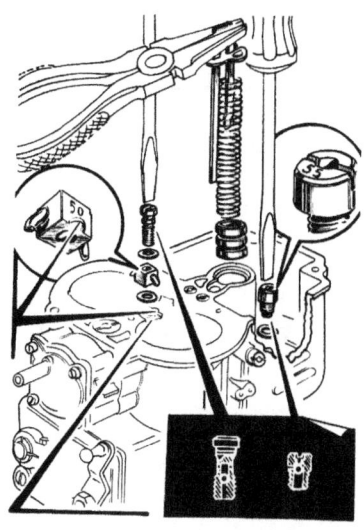

Starting Device (Choke)
1. The exterior housing of the starter is removed as shown in the accompanying drawing. **NOTE:** When reassembling, make sure that the notches on the cover of the DAS unit align.
2. Remove any carbon deposits in the port of the automatic choke.
3. Clean jets and holders in fuel and blow out with compressed air.

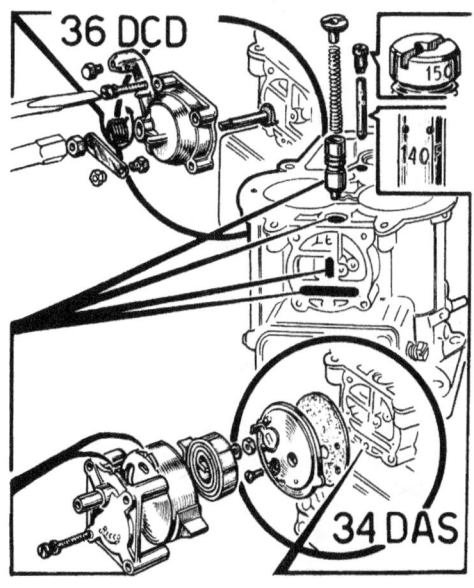

Adjustment of Automatic Choke

Although the automatic choke is pre-set to accommodate most climates it may be necessary to adjust it to accommodate certain operational conditions. If the choke cuts out too soon (lean mixture), turn the thermostatic unit in the direction of the arrow which points toward "rich." If it remains on for too great a period of time (rich mixture), turn it opposite from the arrow direction.

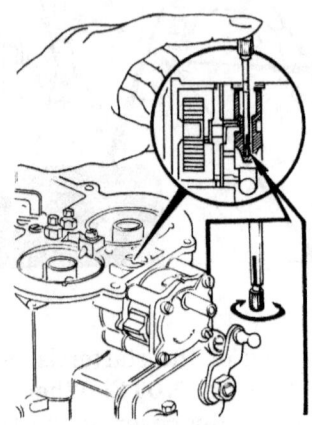

If it is necessary to repair the choke device, a basic adjustment must be made using Weber tool 9620.175.1841. This gauge is inserted in the piston bore and the piston is pushed to the bottom of its travel and a marking on the gauge is aligned with the carburetor body. Then the gauge is left free in the bore and the thermostat box is rotated until the marking denoting ambient air temperature (see illustration) coincides with the thermometer reading (in Centigrade).

Venturis

With the pump delivery jet removed, the venturis can be lifted out with a suitable puller. Weber tools 9610.150.0034 and 0035 are available for this purpose.

Throttle Valves and Shafts

1. Remove the screws securing the throttle plate to the shaft.
2. Remove the plate from the shaft.
3. Loosen the shaft nuts.
4. Remove the bolt and clamp (DAS only).
5. Remove the throttle housing cover screws and withdraw the springs and shafts.

NOTE:

At this point with the carburetor entirely disassembled all

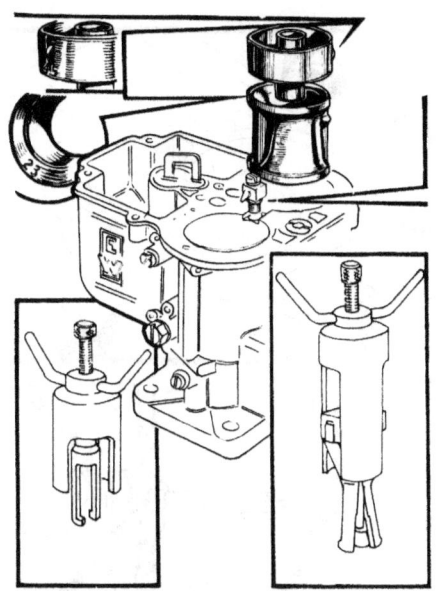

tubes, wells and orifices should be carefully checked, cleaned in fuel and blown out with compressed air. If severely corroded, immersion of the carburetor in carburetor cleaner is advised. Lead plugs for pipes and ducts can be bored out and replaced if necessary.

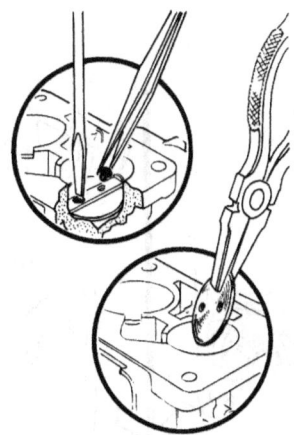

Throttle Shaft Assembly
1. Before assembling the unit, try the various parts together to make sure they operate freely. I.E.: put the shafts and sectors in position without the springs.
2. Fit the nylon bushings with cone facing inward.
3. Put the spring on the primary shaft with the short end to-

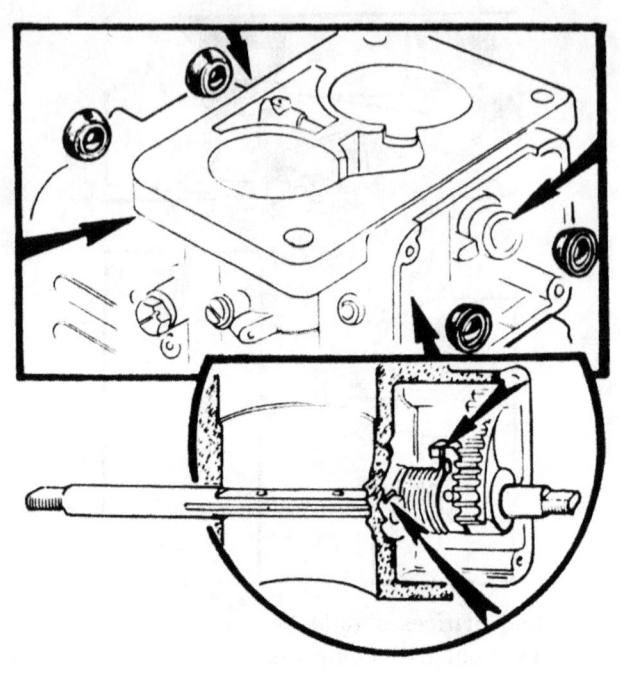

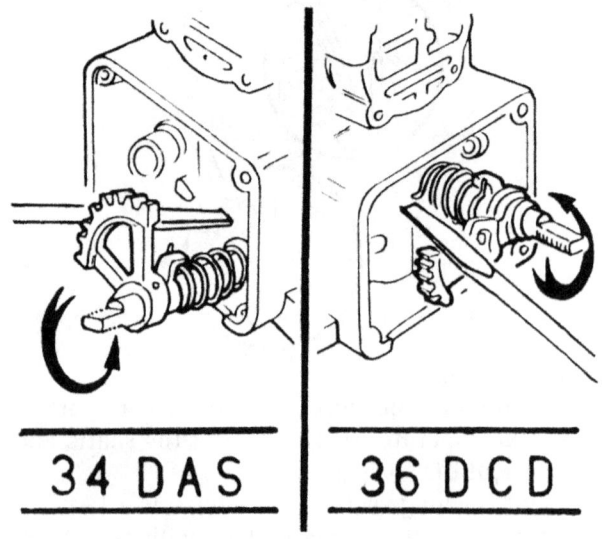

34 DAS | 36 DCD

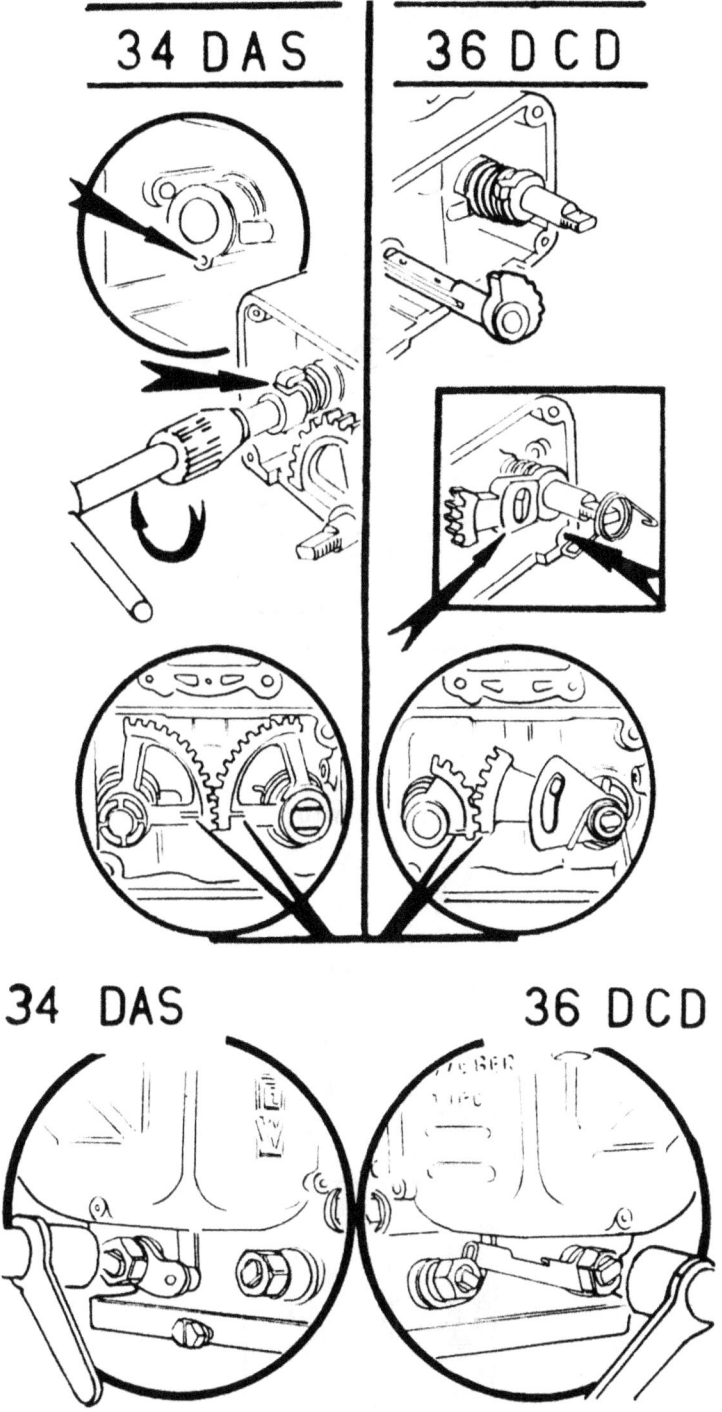

ward the gear sector and introduce the unit into the bore. Be careful that the long end of the spring is placed above the end shank of the carburetor body.

4. Holding the spring in that position, move the shaft outward as much as is required to load the spring then shove it home.

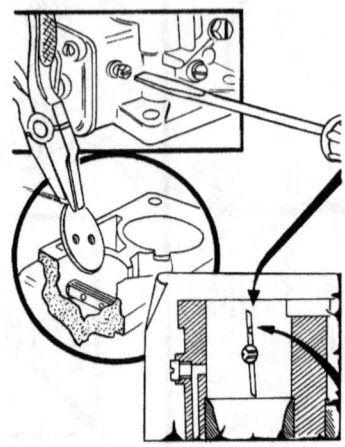

5. Fit the secondary shaft. In the DAS, fit the spring as indicated in the drawing and load it with the special tool 9610.200.0014 or a 14 mm socket. In the DCD, having fitted the secondary shaft, the sector gear with its return spring is then fitted on the primary.

NOTE: Be sure to fit the sectors with scribed lines coinciding.

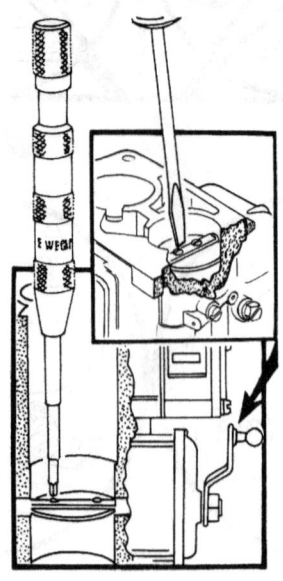

6. Complete the assembly and lock the locking tabs.
7. Slacken the idling setscrew completely.
8. Insert the throttle valves in the slits with beveled edges to contact the walls of the bore. In the DCD check the exact direction of the flaring of the orifice of the secondary.
9. Fit the retaining screws and center the valves.
10. Tighten the screws after checking the freedom of the throttles by working the lever.

NOTE:

For DAS carburetors: To take the play out of the gears proceed as follows:
a. With clamp tightened slightly, close the primary throttle and keep the secondary throttle open.
b. Apply pressure to the secondary throttle plate until it is fully closed.
c. Tighten clamp permanently.

IDLING ADJUSTMENTS

In the DAS begin with ¼ turn from the point of contact for the throttle (idling) setscrew and 1 complete turn for the idling volume control screw. In the DCD, begin with ¼ turn each.

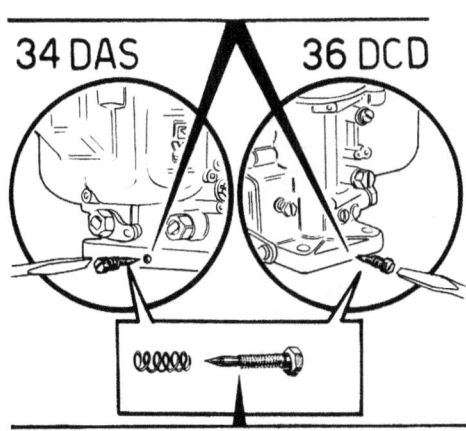

NOTE: There are dozens of Weber carburetors ranging in size from 22 mm to 58 mm and in many confirgurations. To detail each one is beyond the scope of this publication, but catalogs, parts lists and prices are available from the U.S. Weber distributors: GEON, P.O. Box 1000, Woodbury, New York. Phone: (516) 921-8000.

WEBER SPECIAL TOOLS

ATTREZZATURA WEBER PER LA REVISIONE DEI CARBURATORI
WEBER TOOLS FOR OVERHAULING CARBURETORS

1. Attrezzo per montare coprlpolvere
   Tool for mounting dustcover — 9610.315.0957
2. Alesatore per ripassatura condotto valvola avviamento
   Reamer for overhauling starter valve duct — 9600.035.0422
3. Cacciavite grande
   Large screwdriver — 9610.065.0038
   Cacciavite grande
   Large screwdriver — 9610.065.0039
4. Attrezzo per montare cuscinetto nel corpo carburatore
   Tool for mounting bearing on carburetor body — 9610.315.0956
5. Pinza a becco mezzo tondo
   Half-rounded pliers — 9610.535.0034
6. Chiave fissa / Fixed spanner — 9650.120.0001 (6/7)
   Chiave fissa / Fixed spanner — 9650.120.0001 bis (7)
   Chiave fissa / Fixed spanner — 9650.120.0001 bis (8)
   Chiave fissa / Fixed spanner — 9650.120.0001 bis (10)
   Chiave fissa / Fixed spanner — 9650.120.0001 bis (12)
   Chiave fissa / Fixed spanner — 9650.120.0001 bis (14)
   Chiave fissa / Fixed spanner — 9650.120.0001 bis (18/19)
7. Attrezzo per smontare cuscinetto dall'alberino
   Tool for disassembling bearing from spindle — 9610.315.0959
8. Chiave a tubo - esag. 14/15
   Hexagonal box spanner 14/15 — 9650.150.0084
9. Chiave a T - esag. 8-10-12
   Hexagonal T wrench 8-10-12 — 9650.150.0083
10. Chiave speciale esagonale
    Special hexagonal spanner — 9650.150.0088
11. Attrezzo per foratura alberino
    Tool for boring spindle — 9610.020.0507
12. Calibro controllo livellatura galleggiante
    Gauge for checking float levelling — 9620.175.2909
    Calibro controllo livellatura galleggiante
    Gauge for checking float levelling — 9620.175.1990
13. Calibro Ø 1 controllo canalizzazioni
    Gauge Ø 1 for checking ducts — 9620.175.1846
    Calibro Ø 1,5 controllo canalizzazioni
    Gauge Ø 1,5 for checking ducts — 9620.175.1847
    Calibro Ø 2 controllo canalizzazioni
    Gauge Ø 2 for checking ducts — 9620.175.1848
14. Estrattore per diffusori
    Extractor for choke — 9610.150.0034
15. Estrattore per centratori di miscela
    Extractor for auxiliary venturi — 9610.150.0035
16. Filiera Ø 4 x 0,7 / Screw die Ø 4 x 0.7 — 2116.021.0712
    Filiera Ø 5 x 0,8 / Screw die Ø 5 x 0.8 — 2116.029.0712
    Filiera Ø 6 x 1 / Screw die Ø 6 x 1 — 2116.036.0712
    Filiera Ø 7 x 1 / Screw die Ø 7 x 1 — 2116.041.0712
    Filiera Ø 8 x 1 / Screw die Ø 8 x 1 — 2116.047.0712
    Filiera Ø 10 x 1 / Screw die Ø 10 x 1 — 2116.057.0712

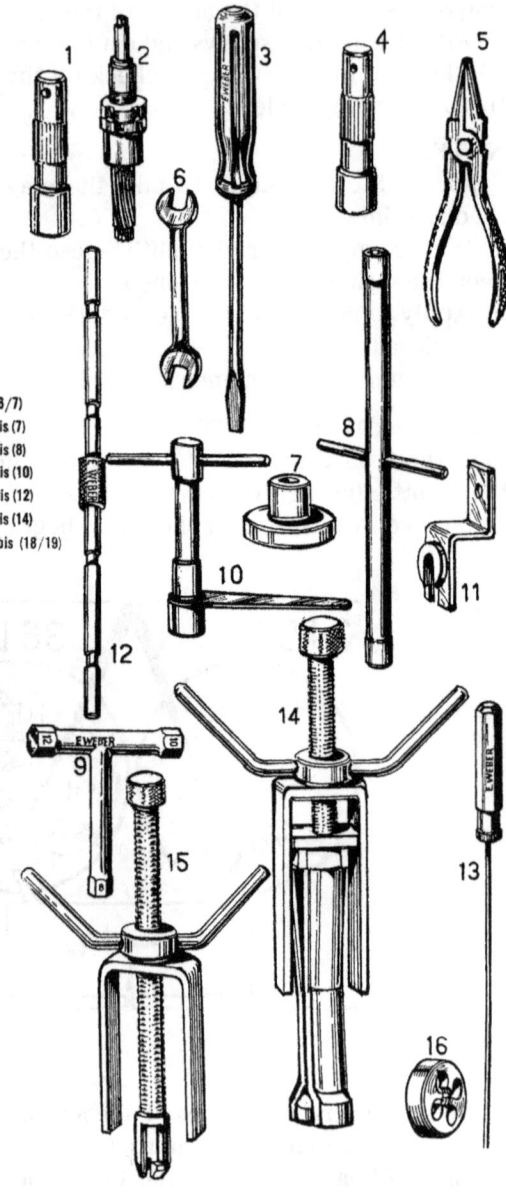

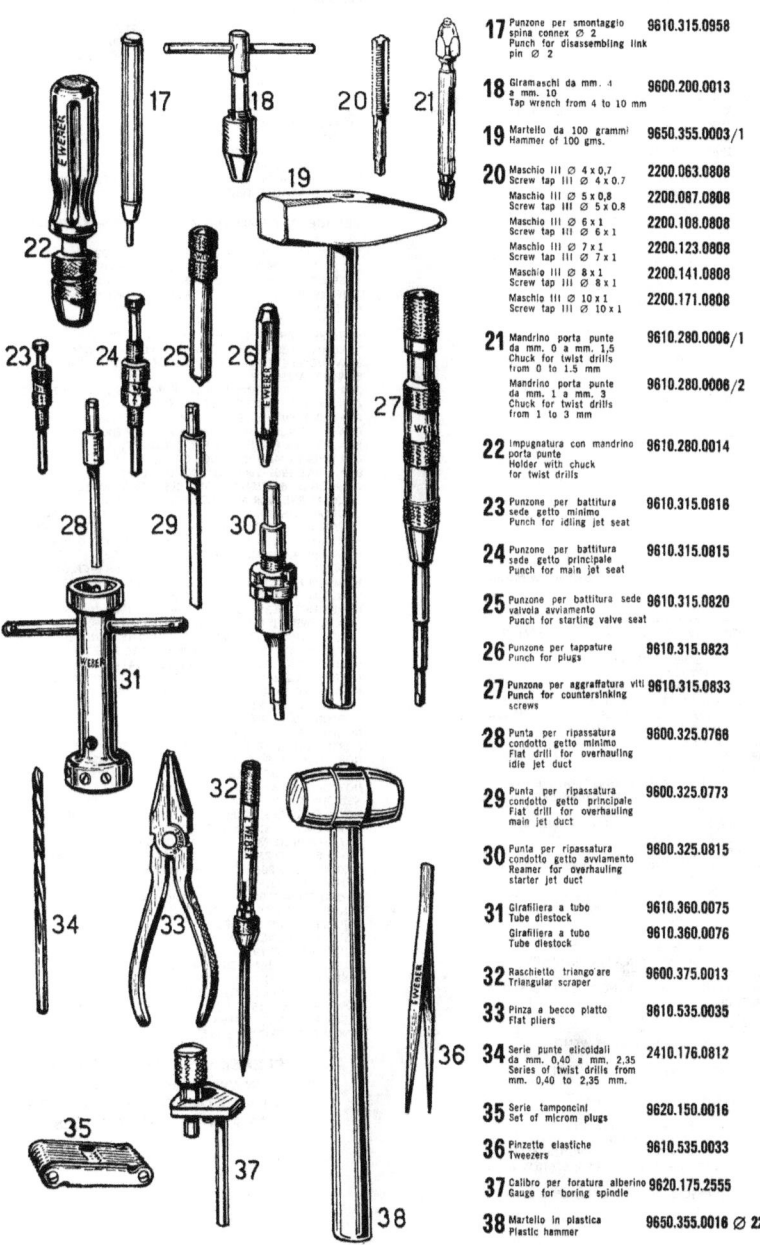

17	Punzone per smontaggio spina connex ⌀ 2 Punch for disassembling link pin ⌀ 2	9610.315.0958
18	Giramaschi da mm. 4 a mm. 10 Tap wrench from 4 to 10 mm	9600.200.0013
19	Martello da 100 grammi Hammer of 100 gms.	9650.355.0003/1
20	Maschio III ⌀ 4 x 0,7 Screw tap III ⌀ 4 x 0.7	2200.063.0808
	Maschio III ⌀ 5 x 0,8 Screw tap III ⌀ 5 x 0.8	2200.087.0808
	Maschio III ⌀ 6 x 1 Screw tap III ⌀ 6 x 1	2200.108.0808
	Maschio III ⌀ 7 x 1 Screw tap III ⌀ 7 x 1	2200.123.0808
	Maschio III ⌀ 8 x 1 Screw tap III ⌀ 8 x 1	2200.141.0808
	Maschio III ⌀ 10 x 1 Screw tap III ⌀ 10 x 1	2200.171.0808
21	Mandrino porta punte da mm. 0 a mm. 1,5 Chuck for twist drills from 0 to 1.5 mm	9610.280.0006/1
	Mandrino porta punte da mm. 1 a mm. 3 Chuck for twist drills from 1 to 3 mm	9610.280.0006/2
22	Impugnatura con mandrino porta punte Holder with chuck for twist drills	9610.280.0014
23	Punzone per battitura sede getto minimo Punch for idling jet seat	9610.315.0818
24	Punzone per battitura sede getto principale Punch for main jet seat	9610.315.0815
25	Punzone per battitura sede valvola avviamento Punch for starting valve seat	9610.315.0820
26	Punzone per tappature Punch for plugs	9610.315.0823
27	Punzone per aggraffatura viti Punch for countersinking screws	9610.315.0833
28	Punta per ripassatura condotto getto minimo Flat drill for overhauling idle jet duct	9600.325.0766
29	Punta per ripassatura condotto getto principale Flat drill for overhauling main jet duct	9600.325.0773
30	Punta per ripassatura condotto getto avviamento Reamer for overhauling starter jet duct	9600.325.0815
31	Girafiliera a tubo Tube diestock	9610.360.0075
	Girafiliera a tubo Tube diestock	9610.360.0076
32	Raschietto triangolare Triangular scraper	9600.375.0013
33	Pinza a becco piatto Flat pliers	9610.535.0035
34	Serie punte elicoidali da mm. 0,40 a mm. 2,35 Series of twist drills from mm. 0,40 to 2,35 mm.	2410.176.0812
35	Serie tamponcini Set of microm plugs	9620.150.0016
36	Pinzette elastiche Tweezers	9610.535.0033
37	Calibro per foratura alberino Gauge for boring spindle	9620.175.2555
38	Martello in plastica Plastic hammer	9650.355.0016 ⌀ 22

AUTOBOOKS WORKSHOP MANUALS

ALFA ROMEO GIULIA 1300, 1600, 1750, 2000 1962-1978 WSM
BMW 1600 1966-1973 WSM
BMW 2000 & 2002 1966-1976 WSM
BMW 2500, 2800, 3.0 & 3.3 1968-1977 WSM
BMW 316, 320, 320i 1975-1977 WSM
BMW 518, 520, 520i 1973-1981 WSM
FIAT 1100, 1100D, 1100R & 1200 1957-1969 WSM
FIAT 124 1966-1974 WSM
FIAT 124 SPORT 1966-1975 WSM
FIAT 125 & 125 SPECIAL 1967-1973 WSM
FIAT 126, 126L, 126 DV, 126/650 & 126/650 DV 1972-1982 WSM
FIAT 127 SALOON, SPECIAL & SPORT, 900, 1050 1971-1981 WSM
FIAT 128 1969-1982 WSM
FIAT 1300, 1500 1961-1967 WSM
FIAT 131 MIRAFIORI 1975-1982 WSM
FIAT 132 1972-1982 WSM
FIAT 500 1957-1973 WSM
FIAT 600, 600D & MULTIPLA 1955-1969 WSM
FIAT 850 1964-1972 WSM
JAGUAR E-TYPE 1961-1972 WSM
JAGUAR MK 1, 2 1955-1969 WSM
JAGUAR S TYPE, 420 1963-1968 WSM
JAGUAR XK 120, 140, 150 MK 7, 8, 9 1948-1961 WSM
LAND ROVER 1, 2 1948-1961 WSM
MERCEDES-BENZ 190 1959-1968 WSM
MERCEDES-BENZ 220/8 1968-1972 WSM
MERCEDES-BENZ 220B 1959-1965 WSM
MERCEDES-BENZ 230 1963-1968 WSM
MERCEDES-BENZ 250 1968-1972 WSM
MERCEDES-BENZ 280 1968-1972 WSM
MG MIDGET TA-TF 1936-1955 WSM
MINI 1959-1980 WSM
MORRIS MINOR 1952-1971 WSM
PEUGEOT 404 1960-1975 WSM
PORSCHE 911 1964-1973 WSM
PORSCHE 911 1970-1977 WSM
RENAULT 16 1965-1979 WSM
RENAULT 8, 10, 1100 1962-1971 WSM
ROVER 3500, 3500S 1968-1976 WSM
SUNBEAM RAPIER, ALPINE 1955-1965 WSM
TRIUMPH SPITFIRE, GT6, VITESSE 1962-1968 WSM
TRIUMPH TR2, TR3, TR3A 1952-1962 WSM
TRIUMPH TR4, TR4A 1961-1967 WSM
VOLKSWAGEN BEETLE 1968-1977 WSM

VELOCEPRESS AUTOMOBILE BOOKS & MANUALS

ABARTH BUYERS GUIDE
AUSTIN-HEALEY 6-CYLINDER WSM
AUSTIN-HEALEY SPRITE & MG MIDGET 1958-1971 WSM
BMW 600 LIMOUSINE FACTORY WSM
BMW 600 LIMOUSINE OWNERS HAND BOOK & SERVICE MANUAL
BMW ISETTA FACTORY WSM
BOOK OF THE CARRERA PANAMERICANA - MEXICAN ROAD RACE
COMPLETE CATALOG OF JAPANESE MOTOR VEHICLES
CORVETTE V8 1955-1962 OWNERS WORKSHOP MANUAL
DIALED IN - THE JAN OPPERMAN STORY
FERRARI 250/GT SERVICE AND MAINTENANCE
FERRARI 308 SERIES BUYER'S AND OWNER'S GUIDE
FERRARI BERLINETTA LUSSO
FERRARI BROCHURES AND SALES LITERATURE 1946-1967
FERRARI BROCHURES AND SALES LITERATURE 1968-1989
FERRARI GUIDE TO PERFORMANCE
FERRARI OPP, MAINTENANCE & SERVICE H/BOOKS 1948-1963
FERRARI OWNER'S HANDBOOK
FERRARI SERIAL NUMBERS PART I - ODD NUMBERS TO 21399
FERRARI SERIAL NUMBERS PART II - EVEN NUMBERS TO 1050
FERRARI SPYDER CALIFORNIA
FERRARI TUNING TIPS & MAINTENANCE TECHNIQUES
HENRY'S FABULOUS MODEL "A" FORD
HOW TO BUILD A FIBERGLASS CAR
HOW TO BUILD A RACING CAR
HOW TO RESTORE THE MODEL 'A' FORD
IF HEMINGWAY HAD WRITTEN A RACING NOVEL
JAGUAR E-TYPE 3.8 & 4.2 WSM
LE MANS 24 (THE BOOK THAT THE FILM WAS BASED ON)
MASERATI BROCHURES AND SALES LITERATURE
MASERATI OWNER'S HANDBOOK
METROPOLITAN FACTORY WSM
MGA & MGB OWNERS HANDBOOK & WSM
OBERT'S FIAT GUIDE
PERFORMANCE TUNING THE SUNBEAM TIGER
PORSCHE 356 1948-1965 WSM
PORSCHE 912 WSM
SOUPING THE VOLKSWAGEN
TRIUMPH TR2, TR3, TR4 1953-1965 WSM
TUNING FOR SPEED (P.E. IRVING)
VEDA ORR'S NEW REVISED HOT ROD PICTORIAL
VOLKSWAGEN TRANSPORTER, TRUCKS, STATION WAGONS WSM
VOLVO 1944-1968 ALL MODELS WSM
WEBER CARBURETORS (EMPHASIS ON ALFA & FIAT)

BROOKLANDS BOOKS & ROAD TEST PORTFOLIOS (RTP)

AC CARS 1904-2009
ALFA ROMEO 1920-1933 ROAD TEST PORTFOLIO
ALFA ROMEO 1934-1940 ROAD TEST PORTFOLIO
BRABHAM RALT HONDA THE RON TAURANAC STORY
BUGATTI TYPE 10 TO TYPE 40 ROAD TEST PORTFOLIO
BUGATTI TYPE 10 TO TYPE 251 ROAD TEST PORTFOLIO
BUGATTI TYPE 41 TO TYPE 55 ROAD TEST PORTFOLIO
BUGATTI TYPE 57 TO TYPE 251 ROAD TEST PORTFOLIO
DELAHAYE ROAD TEST PORTFOLIO
FERRARI ROAD CARS 1946-1956 ROAD TEST PORTFOLIO
FIAT 500 1936-1972 ROAD TEST PORTFOLIO
FIAT DINO ROAD TEST PORTFOLIO
HISPANO SUIZA ROAD TEST PORTFOLIO
HONDA ST1100/ST1300 PAN EUROPEAN 1990-2002 RTP
JAGUAR MK1 & MK2 ROAD TEST PORTFOLIO
LOTUS CORTINA ROAD TEST PORTFOLIO
MV AGUSTA F4 750 & 1000 1997-2007 ROAD TEST PORTFOLIO
TATRA CARS ROAD TEST PORTFOLIO

VELOCEPRESS MOTORCYCLE BOOKS & MANUALS

AJS SINGLES & TWINS 250cc THRU 1000cc 1932-1948 (BOOK OF)
AJS SINGLES 1955-65 350cc & 500cc (BOOK OF)
AJS SINGLES 1945-60 350cc & 500cc MODELS 16 & 18 (BOOK OF)
ARIEL 1939-1960 4 STROKE SINGLES (BOOK OF)
ARIEL LEADER & ARROW 1958-1964 (BOOK OF)
ARIEL MOTORCYCLES 1933-1951 WSM
ARIEL PREWAR MODELS 1932-1939 (BOOK OF)
BMW M/CYCLES R26 R27 (1956-1967) FACTORY WSM
BMW M/CYCLES R50 R50S R60 R69S (1955-1969) FACTORY WSM
BSA BANTAM (BOOK OF)
BSA ALL FOUR-STROKE SINGLES & V-TWINS 1936-1952 (BOOK OF)
BSA OHV & SV SINGLES - 250cc 1954-1970 (BOOK OF)
BSA OHV & SV SINGLES 1945-54 250-600cc (BOOK OF)
BSA OHV SINGLES 350 & 500cc 1955-1967 (BOOK OF)
BSA PRE-WAR MODELS TO 1939 (BOOK OF)
BSA TWINS 1948-1962 (BOOK OF)
BSA TWINS 1962-1969 (SECOND BOOK OF)
CATALOG OF BRITISH MOTORCYCLES (1951 MODELS)
DOUGLAS PRE-WAR ALL MODELS 1929-1939 (BOOK OF)
DOUGLAS POST-WAR ALL MODELS 1948-1957 FACTORY WSM
DUCATI 160cc, 250cc & 350cc OHC MODELS FACTORY WSM
HONDA 50 ALL MODELS UP TO 1970 INC MONKEY & TRAIL (BOOK OF)
HONDA 90 ALL MODELS UP TO 1966 (BOOK OF)
HONDA MOTORCYCLES 125-150 TWINS C/CS/CB/CA WSM
HONDA MOTORCYCLES 250-305 TWINS C/CS/CB WSM
HONDA MOTORCYCLES C100 SUPER CUB WSM
HONDA MOTORCYCLES C110 SPORT CUB 1962-1969 WSM
HONDA TWINS & SINGLES 50cc THRU 305cc 1960-1966 (BOOK OF)
HONDA TWINS ALL MODELS 125cc THRU 450cc UP TO 1968 (BOOK OF)
INDIAN PONYBIKE, BOY RACER & PAPOOSE ILL PARTS LIST & SALES LIT
LAMBRETTA ALL 125 & 150cc MODELS 1947-1957 (BOOK OF)
LAMBRETTA LI & TV MODELS 1957-1970 (SECOND BOOK OF)
MATCHLESS 350 & 500cc SINGLES 1945-1956 (BOOK OF)
MATCHLESS 350 & 500cc SINGLES 1955-1966 (BOOK OF)
NORTON 1932-1947 (BOOK OF)
NORTON 1938-1956 (BOOK OF)
NORTON DOMINATOR TWINS 1955-1965 (BOOK OF)
NORTON MODELS 19, 50 & ES2 1955-1963 (BOOK OF)
NORTON MOTORCYCLES 1957-1970 FACTORY WSM
NORTON PREWAR MODELS 1932-1939 (BOOK OF)
NSU QUICKLY ALL MODELS 1953-1963 (BOOK OF)
ROYAL ENFIELD SINGLES & V TWINS 1937-1953 (BOOK OF)
ROYAL ENFIELD SINGLES 1946-1962 (BOOK OF)
ROYAL ENFIELD 736cc INTERCEPTOR FACTORY WSM
ROYAL ENFIELD 250cc & 350cc SINGLES 1958-1966 (SECOND BOOK OF)
SUZUKI 50cc & 80cc UP TO 1966 (BOOK OF)
SUZUKI T10 1963-1967 FACTORY WSM
SUZUKI T20 & T200 1965-1969 FACTORY WSM
TRIUMPH PRE-WAR MOTORCYCLE 1935-1939 (BOOK OF)
TRIUMPH MOTORCYCLES 1937-1951 WSM
TRIUMPH MOTORCYCLES 1945-1955 FACTORY WSM
TRIUMPH TWINS 1956-1969 (BOOK OF)
VELOCETTE ALL SINGLES & TWINS 1925-1970 (BOOK OF)
VESPA 1951-1961 (BOOK OF)
VESPA 125 & 150cc & GS MODELS 1955-1963 (SECOND BOOK OF)
VESPA 90, 125 & 150cc 1963-1972 (THIRD BOOK OF)
VESPA GS & SS 1955-1968 (BOOK OF)
VINCENT MOTORCYCLES 1935-1955 WSM

PLEASE VISIT OUR WEBSITE
www.VelocePress.com
FOR A DETAILED DESCRIPTION
OF ANY OF THESE TITLES

www.ingramcontent.com/pod-product-compliance
Lightning Source LLC
Chambersburg PA
CBHW070543170426
43200CB00011B/2537